This book belongs to:

_____

My Favourite
Company
Pty Ltd

HISTORY OF MALAYSIA
A Children's Encyclopedia

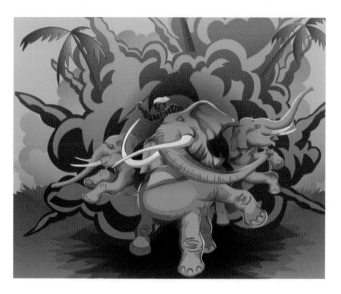

We are grateful for the generous support of:

MAA Assurance
MALAYSIAN ASSURANCE ALLIANCE BERHAD

Note for Readers: *Both spellings of 'Terengganu'
and 'Trengganu' are used in this book. The former is
the modern spelling of that state.*

Printed in Malaysia
ISBN 978-0-646-49827-0

HISTORY OF MALAYSIA
A Children's Encyclopedia

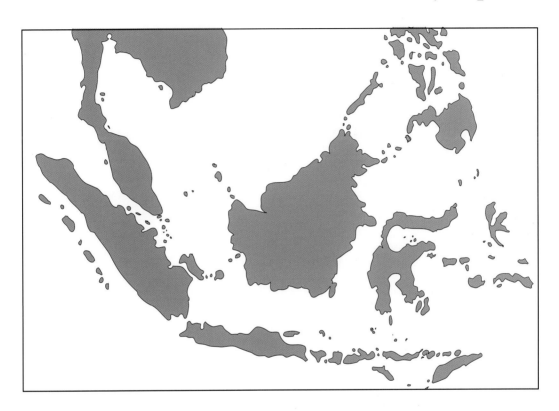

Contents

This musical instrument is a Nepiri which forms part of the Nobat, or royal band. The old custom was that whenever a person heard the sound of the Nepiri, he or she must stop all activities and sit down as if the Ruler himself was before them.

Maps of the Region

SIAM

CAMBODIA

Patani

Kedah

Kelantan

Aceh Pasai

Trengganu

MALAY
PENINSULA

Perak

Selangor

Pahang

Rembau

Melaka

Johor

Siak

Kampar

Riau-Lingga

Minangkabau

Jambi

Palembang

SUMATRA

JAVA

N

W

E

S

Pre-Colonial South-East Asia

PHILIPPINES

Sulu

BRUNEI

SPICE ISLANDS

CELEBES

Majapahit

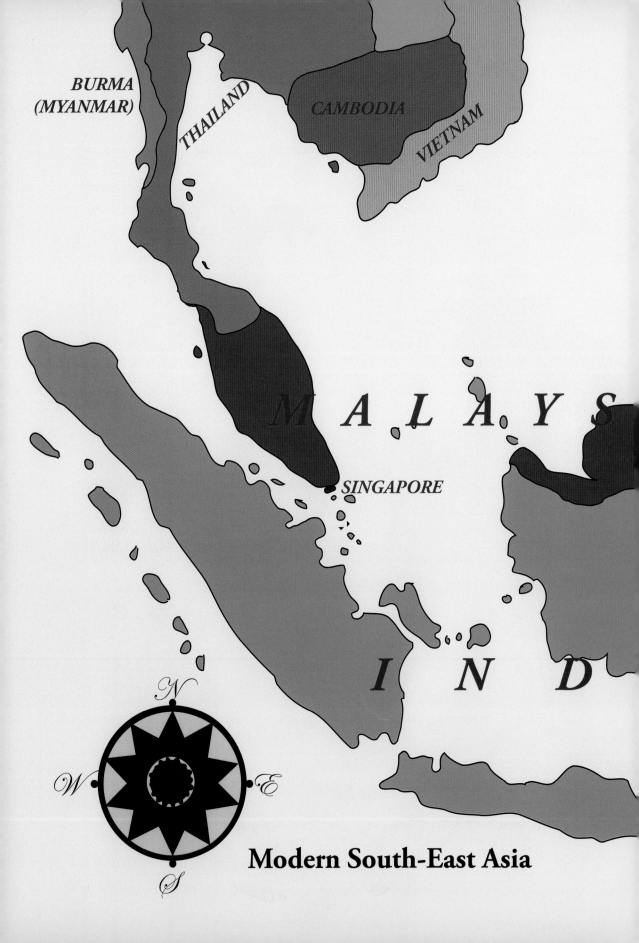

BURMA
(MYANMAR)

THAILAND

CAMBODIA

VIETNAM

M A L A Y S

SINGAPORE

I N D

N

W   E

S

Modern South-East Asia

This is a sirih set made of silver and gold, perhaps made for a Ruler's own use. Sirih is a betel vine. In Malay custom, the leaf is wrapped around areca nut and lime and chewed as a past time.

A to Z to History

This part of the book contains many topics. Some have a common link. For example, in *Siamese Invasion of Kedah*, *Aceh Attacks*, *Rebellion Against British Rule* and the *Second World War* you can discover the wars fought. Other topics like *Borneo*, *Chinese*, *Indians*, *Minangkabaus*, *Bugis* and *Orang Asli* you'll find out about the country's different peoples.

As Malaysia's history spans thousands of years, this section is colour coded. It is divided it into four periods, each with a colour.

Can you answer some of the questions here? If you like quizzes, have a go at those in the Question & Answer section on page 109.

What were these ornamental flowers used for?

Whose logo was this?

"In this A to Z section you will discover many different topics across a time scale of thousands of years."

Each topic is linked to others. Follow me to these topics and you'll discover so much more!

> "Each colour coded period begins and ends with an important event in Malaysia's history"

Why was this man seeking revenge? And against whom?

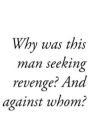	***Early History***	1st century to 1511
	Middle History	1511 to 1824
	Early Modern History	1824 to 1939
	Modern History	1939 to Present Day

In the above chart, the period we call *Early History* ends with the Portuguese invasion of Melaka in 1511. This is followed by *Middle History* which concludes with the Anglo-Dutch treaty. The next period, *Early Modern History*, ends with the Second World War. The period *Modern History* then begins and continues until the present day. By noting the main colour used on each page, you can tell which period of history you are examining.

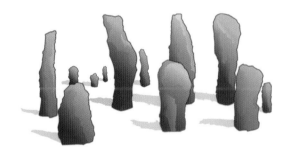

What are these mysterious standing stones?

Aceh Attacks

In the early 16th Century, the kingdom of Aceh, located in north Sumatra, conquered its neighbour, the kingdom of Pasai.

After the fall of Melaka to the Portuguese, Muslim traders went to Aceh which made the kingdom wealthy. With a strong fighting force and a zeal to spread Islam, the Acehnese captured much of Sumatra.

Led by Sultan Iskandar Muda, it conquered Pahang, Kedah and Perak sending thousands of its inhabitants back as slaves. The kingdom of Riau-Johor was under constant Acehnese attack.

Portuguese Melaka was the only power that stood in the way of the Acehnese. The Portuguese garrison fought off a massive Acehnese attack in 1629. In a Portuguese counterattack, with support from the kingdom of Riau-Johor, the Acehnese suffered terrible losses. From then on, the Achenese empire began to decline.

Even so, when the Dutch arrived in Sumatra two and half centuries later, they fought for 30 years to conquer Aceh.

"... there were in Aceh 22,000 slaves captured in these invasions. Of this number only about 1,500 survived the ordeal."

**Barbara Watson Andaya &
Leonard Y. Andaya**
A History of Malaysia

A small Malay cannon

Key Dates

1524 - Aceh conquers the neighbouring kingdom of Pasai

1540 - Riau-Johor sinks 160 Acehnese ships

1617-1620 Aceh captures Pahang, Kedah and Perak, taking slaves

1629 - Aceh attacks Portuguese Melaka but is defeated in a counterattack

A Malay ship used during this period

Captured Sultans

Aceh attacked Riau-Johor in 1613 and Sultan Alauddin was taken to Aceh where he died a prisoner. Riau-Johor's next ruler was constantly on the run after the Acehnese destroyed his palace in Lingga. When Aceh captured Perak, the Perak Sultan's widow and children were taken to Aceh. The eldest son became the husband of the queen of Aceh. Four years later, he became the sultan of Aceh and sent his younger brother back to Perak to become its ruler.

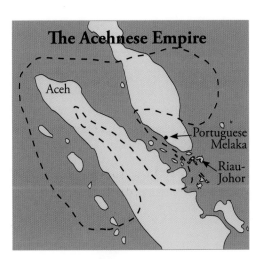

The Acehnese Empire

Aceh

Portuguese Melaka

Riau-Johor

Enemies Unite

As Aceh grew in power, the kingdom of Riau-Johor had to defend itself. At times, Riau-Johor and Portuguese Melaka had to fight together against their common enemy, Aceh. The Sultan even made a state visit to Portuguese Melaka.

Attack on Portuguese Melaka

Using a massive force of 20,000 warriors and 200 ships, Aceh attacked Portuguese Melaka. The Acehnese fought their way almost into the centre of the city. Portuguese ships then arrived from Goa and together with ships from Riau-Johor, they counterattacked. The Acehnese suffered heavy losses. Between 10,000 and 20,000 Achenese were killed. From then on Aceh's power declined.

Achenese gravestone

Find Out More

Melaka Empire
Portuguese Invasion
Dutch Influence

17

Borneo

For centuries the kingdom of Brunei ruled the west coast of Borneo. In the 9th century, China called the kingdom "P'o-ni". When Melaka fell to the Portuguese, Brunei became wealthier because its Muslim traders fled to Brunei to trade.

By the 18th century, Brunei had grown weak due to competition from the kingdom of Sulu. When an English adventurer, James Brooke, brought peace to the Sarawak river, the Sultan rewarded him and made him the Rajah of Sarawak. Over the years, Brooke bought more land from the money-strapped kingdom.

The Sultan sold his other territory, North Borneo, to Charles Moses. Eventually, North Borneo fell into the hands of the Chartered Company.

After the Second World War, Britain took control of Sarawak and North Borneo. Later, Sarawak and North Borneo (renamed Sabah) joined the Federation of Malaysia.

The Hornbill is a native bird of Borneo

British Protectorates

By 1905 Brunei, Sarawak and North Borneo were protected by the British. The Sultan of Brunei accepted a British Resident and this saved his weak kingdom. Britain did this to stop other European powers from interfering in these territories.

Sabah

Moses, the Baron and Dent

The kingdom of Brunei had ruled North Borneo for centuries but by 1865 it had become weak and needed money. So an American called Charles Moses bought North Borneo from the Sultan. As Moses's business had failed, he sold it to an Austrian, Baron von Overbeck. Ultimately, an Englishman, Alfred Dent, became the owner of North Borneo. Because the kingdom of Sulu claimed to own the north coast of Borneo, Dent bought North Borneo again, this time from the Sultan of Sulu. Dent then formed the Chartered Company to rule North Borneo.

The Chartered Company

After becoming owner of North Borneo, Dent formed the British North Borneo Company. It was commonly called the "Chartered Company" The company managed and exploited North Borneo's resources. It banned slavery and head hunting. It made money from selling North Borneo's timber. After the Second World War, the company gave up its rights to North Borneo and Labuan to Britain. This was because Britain could help with Sabah's reconstruction.

The People of Sabah

The largest population in Sabah are the Kadazans and Dusuns. They live mostly on the West Coast of Sabah. Making a livelihood from farming, the Kadazans live on the plains whereas the Dusuns live on the hilly areas of Sabah. Other peoples in Sabah include the Murut, who were hunters, the Bajaus, who were sea gypsies, and the Ilanuns, who were pirates.

Kadazan women

Sarawak

Portrait of James Brooke

The White Rajah

James Brooke, who was brought up in India, was an adventurer. He sailed to the Malay peninsula and then to Borneo and the Sarawak river. In Sarawak, the Bidayuhs, Ibans and Malays were at war. With superior cannons on his ship and good negotiating skills, James Brooke brought peace. As a reward the Crown Prince of Brunei, Raja Muda Hassim, made him its ruler and Brooke became the Rajah of Sarawak. The war-like Ibans fought against the new White Rajah's rule but were defeated. Over the years Brooke's kingdom grew in size as he bought more and more land from Brunei, eventually creating Sarawak's borders today.

End of the White Rajahs

When James Brooke died, his nephew, Charles Brooke, become the second White Rajah. The third White Rajah was Charles's son, Vyner Brooke. The rule of the Brooke dynasty ended after the Second World War. The British government took over the state to help with its reconstruction. The White Rajahs, beginning with James Brooke, had ruled Sarawak for more than a hundred years.

The People of Sarawak

Unlike the Malay peninsula, a large population of indigenous people lived in Sarawak. The indigenous people were diverse though most of them were Bidayuhs (Land Dayaks) and Ibans (Sea Dayaks). The Bidayuhs were an interior people. Their livelihood was based on shifting agriculture and farming. The Ibans were fearsome warriors, pirates and practised headhunting. Other indigenous Sarawakians include the Melanaus, Kedayans, Kalabits, Punan and Muruts. Although originally animists, most of the indigenous peoples are now Christian.

Dayak warriors

Find Out More

British Control
Malaysia and Confrontation
Rebellion Against British Rule

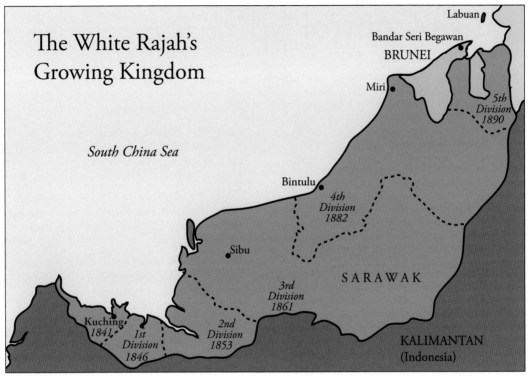

From the modest area of Kuching in 1841, James Brooke's new country expanded until it reached its present size in 1890.

Key Dates

1841 - James Brooke becomes Rajah of Sarawak

1877 - Alfred Dent buys North Borneo from Brunei

1881 - North Borneo Chartered Company is established

1888 - Sarawak, North Borneo and Brunei become British protectorates

1946 - Sarawak and North Borneo become British Crown Colonies

"All day, hawkers piled their wares, gongs beat in the mosque ... At night there was the eternal chorus of tree-frogs, bull frogs, and strange beetles. The magic of it possessed me, sight, sound and sense; there was in this abundant land everything for which my heart had yearned"

Sylvia Lady Brooke
Wife of the Last Rajah of Sarawak
Queen of the Head-hunters

British Control

Like the Portuguese and the Dutch before them, the British came to South East Asia to trade. They started their own trading settlements with their first foothold in Penang followed by another in Singapore.

Under the Anglo-Dutch Treaty, Holland and England divided the Malay archipelago between themselves. The British took over Dutch Melaka and so the British colonies of Penang, Singapore and Melaka became known as the Straits Settlements.

Britain first got involved in the affairs of a Malay kingdom with the Low Treaty which brought Perak under British protection.

Britain went a step further with the Pangkor Treaty when it boldly intervened in Perak's government and placed a British Resident in that state. Soon Selangor, Pahang and Negri Sembilan too had British Residents. Britain came to dominate the other Malay kingdoms and eventually all of the peninsula came under British rule.

Anglo-Dutch Treaty

Britain and Holland were rivals and both had settlements and influence on the Malay peninsula and Sumatra. Under the Anglo-Dutch Treaty, the Dutch gave up its influence on the Malay peninsula. The Malay peninsula was left to Britian who then took over Dutch Melaka. The British, in turn, gave up its influence on Sumatra to the Dutch who then took over of the British settlement of Bencoolen. This treaty split up the kingdom of Riau-Johor. It also separated the close ties between Sumatra and the Malay peninsula. The treaty eventually created the borders between the two modern nations of Malaysia and Indonesia.

Low Treaty

Britain sent Captain James Low to Perak with forty sepoys and a small warship to defend it against the Siamese, who had invaded Kedah. He then signed a treaty with the ruler of Perak. With this treaty, Low promised that the British would defend Perak against its enemies. Perak, in turn, promised to have no dealings with Siam or any other state except the British. The Perak Ruler also gave the British several islands, including Pangkor, and a strip on the mainland called the Dindings.

British officials meeting in Kuala Lumpur in 1903

Pangkor Treaty

The tin mine wars in Perak caused British traders in the Straits Settlements to lose money. Britain wanted to end the war in Perak so that it could trade without disruption. On a ship anchored off Pangkor island, Sir Andrew Clarke, the British Governor of the Straits Settlements, appointed Raja Abdullah as the ruler of Perak. However, the new ruler had to accept a British Resident who would be in charge of the kingdom's affairs.

At this time, Selangor too was troubled by its own tin mine war. So its ruler, Sultan Abdul Samad, agreed to a British Resident. This was followed by Sungei Ujong, a state in Negri Sembilan, which also accepted a British Resident.

The East India Company's flag

Raja Abdullah of Perak

Federated Malay States

After Perak, Sungei Ujong and Selangor had accepted British Residents, Pahang and the other Negri Sembilan states soon did the same. The British grouped Perak, Selangor, Pahang and Negri Sembilan into, what it called, the Federated Malay States. The British directly controlled the affairs of these states.

Unfederated Malay States

Kedah, Perlis, Kelantan and Terengganu were controlled by Siam. Under the Treaty of Bangkok, the Siamese passed suzerainty of these states to the British. These states, including Johor, did not take British Residents and so were not under direct British control. The British called these kingdoms the Unfederated Malay States.

British Malaya

The Straits Settlements, the Federated Malay States and the Unfederated Malay States became known as "British Malaya". The term sometimes also includes the British possessions in Borneo, including Sarawak, Labuan and North Borneo.

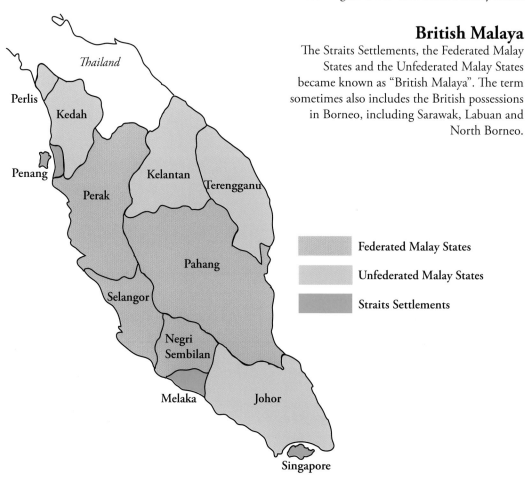

Federated Malay States

Unfederated Malay States

Straits Settlements

British Borneo

James Brooke, his nephew, and grand nephew were the White Rajahs of Sarawak. They ran Sarawak as their own kingdom. As for Sabah, which was then called North Borneo, it was controlled by the Chartered Company which had bought the territory from the kingdom of Brunei. After the Second World War, to help rebuild these states, the British government took over Sabah and Sarawak.

Key Dates

1786 - Francis Light starts a British settlement in Penang

1819 - Stamford Raffles starts a British settlement in Singapore

1824 - Anglo-Dutch Treaty: Britain takes control of Melaka

1826 - Low Treaty in Perak. Penang, Singapore and Melaka become the Straits Settlements

1874 - Pangkor Treaty. Perak, Selangor and Sungei Ujong take British Residents

1896 - Perak, Selangor, Pahang and Negri Sembilan become the Federated Malay States

1909 - Treaty of Bangkok. Kedah, Perlis. Kelantan, Terengganu and Johor become the Unfederated Malay States.

British Adminstrators

The British Administrators ran British Malaya. These included Sir Andrew Clarke and Sir Frederick Weld, both were Governors of the Straits Settlements. Each state was governed by a British Resident. The first British Residents were Sir Hugh Clifford in Pahang, Martin Lister in Negri Sembilan, J.G Davidson in Selangor and James Birch in Perak. When

Birch was killed, Sir Hugh Low became the second British Resident in Perak. Perhaps the most influential British admistrator was Frank Sweetenham (pictured right). He was the first Resident General of the Federated Malay States and later Governor.

"In the larger towns ... it is possible to go shopping during the morning, or to visit friends, but in the smaller stations or on estates or mines, life is apt to be monotonous ... House servants are usually either Chinese or Tamil. The general staff will in general consist of a houseboy, a water carrier, a cook, a gardener, a chauffeur and perhaps an ayah *(if* Chinese amah) *or two."*

Handbook to British Malaya (1927)

Find Out More

Rebellion Against British Rule
Tin Mine Wars
Independence

Bugis

The Bugis are a people that first came to the Malay peninsula from the island known as the Celebes, which today is called 'Sulawesi'.

In the south of the island, there live the Torajans in the highlands and the Bugis in the lowlands. In the north, there are the Filipino-descended Minahasans.

Three hundred years ago, because of wars, many Bugis sailed away from Sulawasi to find a better life. They travelled to many places to settle including Borneo, Selangor and Negri Sembilan. As a people, the Bugis were good sailors, traders and fighters.

In the 18th century they took control of the old Malay kingdom of Riau-Johor and started their own kingdom in Selangor. Their rivals were the Dutch in Melaka against whom they fought two wars.

The Bugis are part of the wider Malay community in modern Malaysia.

"The Bugis are known by their neighbours for their fierce character and sense of honour, which sometimes result in violence; and yet they are the most hospitable and amicable peoples and the most faithful in their friendships."

Christian Pelras
The Bugis

From the late 17th Century, the Bugis migrated from the Celebes to Linggi, Kelang and Selangor on the Malay peninsula. They also migrated to Borneo.

Capturing Riau-Johor

After Sultan Mahmud of Riau-Johor was murdered, Bendahara Abdul Jalil became the new sultan. Because he was not of royal blood, many locals did not support him. Raja Kechil, a Minangkabau from Sumatra, claimed to be the dead sultan's son. With the Sea Gypsies deserting Riau-Johor and fighting for him, Raja Kechil won the battle. The Yamtuan Muda, the Sultan's brother, then ran amok and killed his own wife and children. The Bugis then joined the conflict. Led by Daeng Parani from Selangor, they fought Raja Kechil on land and sea and drove him out of Riau-Johor.

New Under Kings

Because the Bugis were not regarded as Malay, they asked Sulaiman, a son of Sultan Abdul Jalil, to become ruler. The Bugis leader then made his brother, Daeng Merewah, the new Yamtuan Muda or Under King. The Bugis Under King would wield true power whilst the Malay rulers would be figureheads. For the following 200 years the Bugis Yamtuan Mudas would be the power behind the throne.

"The Yang DiPertuan Besar [Sultan Sulaiman] is like a woman. When food is given to him, he may eat. And the Yang DiPertuan Muda is like her man, should any question arise, it is he who decides on it."

Silsilah Melayu dan Bugis

First Bugis-Dutch War

The Bugis and the Malays in Riau-Johor's captial in Bintan argued constantly. So in 1753, the Bugis sailed away and began their own trading centre in Linggi, now in Negri Sembilan. As the Bugis were good traders, ships soon travelled to Linggi to trade and Bintan lost its wealth. In revenge, Sultan Sulaiman asked the Dutch to help him defeat the Bugis. But the Bugis uncovered the plan and attacked the Dutch, almost capturing Dutch Melaka. Eventually, the Dutch won. Sultan Sulaiman allowed the defeated Bugis leader, Daeng Kemboja, to return to Bintan. This proved to be a terrible mistake.

A Dutch ship

Second Bugis-Dutch War

Hostilities began when the Bugis and Dutch argued over the cargo of a seized English ship. In frustration, the Bugis leader, Raja Haji, attacked vessels in the Melaka Straits. The Dutch tried to blockade Bintan but failed. The Bugis, supported by Selangor and Rembau, then attacked Dutch Melaka. Vessels from Holland then arrived and defeated the Bugis. Raja Haji was killed and the Bugis fled to Bintan. The Dutch then captured Bintan and took control of Riau-Johor. Sultan Mahmud remained as sultan but the new Dutch resident, David Ruhde, held the real power. Power in the old kingdom of Riau-Johor had passed from the Malays to the Bugis and now to the Dutch.

Three Poisoned Kings?

After the First Bugis-Dutch War, Daeng Kemboja and the Bugis returned to Bintan. That same year the elderly Sultan Sulaiman died. The following two sultans, his son and grandson, died the year after. The next sultan was the infant Sultan Mahmud. Many Malays believed that their three sultans were poisoned by the Bugis. With no strong Sultan to challenge them the Bugis once again became powerful in the kingdom of Riau-Johor.

Cannons were one of the main weapons used during the conflicts

Find Out More

Riau-Johor
Dutch Influence
Pahang Civil War

Bugis Brothers

Although migrants from the Celebes, the descendants of Daeng Relaga would wield great power on the Malay peninsula. They would rule the old kingdom of Riau-Johor and begin a new sultanate in Selangor. "Daeng" is a Bugis title of nobility.

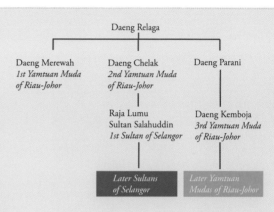

Daeng Relaga

Daeng Merewah
1st Yamtuan Muda of Riau-Johor

Daeng Chelak
2nd Yamtuan Muda of Riau-Johor

Daeng Parani

Raja Lumu
Sultan Salahuddin
1st Sultan of Selangor

Daeng Kemboja
3rd Yamtuan Muda of Riau-Johor

Later Sultans of Selangor

Later Yamtuan Mudas of Riau-Johor

Raja Lumu's great grandson, Sultan Abdul Samad (seated) and his followers

New Sultanate of Selangor

Around 1680, the Bugis first arrived in Selangor to start a new settlement. They became powerful and even captured the kingdom of Riau-Johor where they installed their own Yamtuan Muda or Under King. The Yamtuan Muda's family from Riau-Johor then ruled Selangor. The Bugis in Selangor wished to break away from Riau-Johor. So Selangor's chief, Raja Lumu, travelled to Perak and there its ruler installed him as Sultan. Raja Lumu took the name Sultan Salehuddin and became the first Sultan of Selangor. His descendants rule Selangor today.

Key Dates

1721 - Bugis from Selangor capture Riau-Johor.

1758 - First Bugis-Dutch war

1766 - Sultan Salehuddin Shah becomes first Sultan of Selangor

1784 - Second Bugis-Dutch war

1785 - David Ruhde becomes first Dutch Resident of Riau-Johor

Map of Selangor and surrounding states

Chinese

For centuries, the Chinese had visited the early kingdoms on the Malay peninsula and Sumatra. They only came to live permanently in the Malay peninsula during the period of the Melaka Empire in the 15th century. Their descendants are known as Babas and adopted their own unique culture.

More than three centuries later, in the 1850s, many Chinese from southern China moved to the British Straits Settlements. The Straits Settlements were the British colonies of Penang, Melaka and Singapore. These arrivals were know as Straits Chinese.

When miners were needed to work in the tin mines on the Malay peninsula, businessmen from the Straits Settlements brought in Chinese workers from China. Because of poverty in China, thousands of them arrived in the Malay peninsula. They worked in tin mines as coolies.

Through hard work and enterprise some poor Chinese became rich.

"The Sultan [of Melaka] was astonished to behold the beauty of the Princess of China ... and the raja appointed the hill without the fort for their residence and the Chinese formed a well at the foot of this China hill."

John Leyden's Malay Annals

Red lanterns at Chinese New Year

*A Chinese ship,
known as a "junk"*

Piecemeal Migration

Although most Chinese migrated to the Malay peninsula during the 19th century, there was also piecemeal migration a century earlier. When the Dutch returned to Bintan in 1788, they found 5000 Chinese from Canton and Amoy who worked on gambier plantations. In Kelantan there were Chinese goldminers from Kwantung. In Brunei, there was a settlement of Chinese pepper planters. In Selangor, settlers from Kwantung and Fukien were working the tin mines well before the later arrivals.

Yap Ah Loy

Kapitan China

The Kapitan China were Chinese headmen in charge of the Chinese tin mines and the Chinese community in their area. They were recognised as such by the Malay ruler. One famous Kapitan China was Yap Ah Loy who started mines in the Kuala Lumpur area.

Chinese Dialects

The dialects the Chinese brought with them included:

- Hokkien from Fukien
- Teochew and Cantonese from Kwantung
- Hakka from the mountain areas of Kwantung, Kwangsi and Fukkien
- Hainanese from Hainan Island
- Other dialects included Houkchew, Kwongsai, Henghua and Hokchia.

Tin Mines and Coolies

Tin was in big demand overseas and jobs in the mines were plentiful. Migrants from China, known as "sinkeh" or "newcomers", came to work the tin mines on the Malay peninsula. As they had to pay to be brought over, these coolies had to work off their debt. This was difficult especially when they had to buy food and other necessities from their employers. This only increased their debt. Sometimes the coolies would join a secret society, like the Ghee Hin or Hai San, for protection.

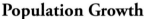

Loke Yew

Population Growth

In 2004 the Chinese made up 24% of the Malaysian population. The table below shows the population growth.

Year	Population	Location
1871	104,600	Straits Settlements
1901	301,463	Malaya & Singapore
1941	2,418,615	Malaya & Singapore: 44% of the population
2004	735,038	Malaysia: 24% of the population

Source: Guy Hunter. South East Asia: Race, Culture, Nation

Loke Yew

Loke Yew was born in Southern China and at the age of 13 moved to Singapore. He developed tin mines and ventured into agriculture. He also maintained railways and collected taxes for the British. He became business partners with another renown businessman, Thamboosamy Pillai. Although hugely successful, Loke Yew was illiterate. He died in 1917.

Roots and Religion

The Chinese that arrived in Malaya during the 19th century were mainly from South China. Their homelands were the provinces of Fukien, Kwantung and Kwangsi. The Chinese migrants brought with them their different religions. They were Confucion, Taoist, Buddhist, Christians and Muslims.

Joss stick and oranges at a Taoist altar

A Baba family

Babas

When Paramesvara, Melaka's first ruler, married princess Hang Li Po she brought an entourage of 500 handmaidens and many followers to Melaka. They made their home in what is now known as Bukit China. The Chinese men married local Malay women and created their own culture. They are today known as Babas or Peranakan Chinese ("Peranakan" means "locally born").

The Nyonyas (Baba women) wear sarongs smiliar to those worn by Malay women. The Babas may not speak Chinese at all but rather Baba Malay which is a mix of Malay and Hokkien, a Chinese dialect. Their cuisine is a delicious mix of Chinese and Malay food.

"It has been said that Babas are Chinese in spirit and tradition but Malay in form. This observation is made especially because Nyonyas wear sarong like Malay women do. Babas speaking little or no Chinese at all but Baba Malay ..."

Felix Chia
The Babas

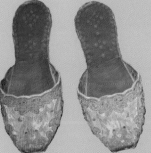

Slippers worn by Nyonyas

Find Out More

Tin Mine Wars
Indians
Melaka Empire

Dutch Influence

Since the early 17th century, the Dutch had been Portugal's trading rival. The Dutch had started the Dutch United East India Company or VOC.

From their trading centre in Batavia (today it is called Jakarta), the VOC felt threatened by the Portuguese. With Riau-Johor support, the Dutch conquered Portuguese Melaka. The VOC made Batavia its main trading centre and Melaka became less important.

The Bugis-controlled kingdom of Riau-Johor was also a rival trading centre to Melaka. The Bugis fought and lost two wars against the Dutch. Eventually Riau-Johor came under Dutch rule.

Under the Anglo-Dutch Treaty, the Dutch left the Malay peninsula and the western part of Borneo to the British. This treaty eventually created the borders between Malaysia and Indonesia.

VOC emblem taken from a Dutch cannon. "VOC" stands for Vereenigne Oostindische Compagnie or the Dutch East India Company.

Key Dates

1602 - The VOC is formed

1619 - The Dutch establish a base at Jakarta

1641 - The Dutch capture Melaka

1759 - Britain temporarily takes possession of Melaka

1824 - Anglo-Dutch Treaty

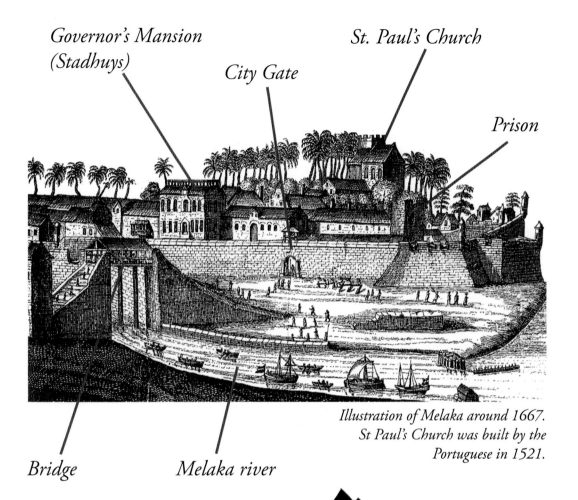

Governor's Mansion
(Stadhuys)

City Gate

St. Paul's Church

Prison

Bridge

Melaka river

*Illustration of Melaka around 1667.
St Paul's Church was built by the
Portuguese in 1521.*

The Siege of Melaka

In August 1640, the Dutch joined forces with Riau-Johor to attack Portuguese Melaka. The Portuguese fought bravely and held out for nearly two years. During the seige, the starving Melakans and Portuguese had to eat dogs and cats. Many of the Dutch died from disease. On 13 January, 650 Dutch soldiers, armed with grenades, spears, cutlasses and ladders, made a final attack and the Portuguese surrendered.

A Dutch rifle

Dutch Buildings

After capturing Melaka from the Portuguese, the Dutch quickly repaired the walls and fortifications in case of attack. Where the Portuguese Governor's house once stood, they built a new mansion for the Dutch Governor. Completed around 1650, it is now known as the Stadhuys (Town Hall). This was followed over a hundred years later with the completion of a church called Christ Church.

A Dutch grave stone at the Portuguese fort in Melaka.

"We must continue to remember that the Johor people contributed substantially towards the conquest of Melaka. Without their help we would never have become master of that strong place."

Antonio van Diemen
Dutch Governor-General

Perak Tin

Perak was rich in tin. But the kingdom was overshadowed by its more powerful neighbours like Aceh, Siam and the Portuguese. When the Dutch captured Melaka, Perak sought protection from the Dutch, particularly against Siam. To protect Perak, the VOC built a fort on Pangkor opposite the Dindings River. In return, the Dutch wanted to control all of Perak's tin but Perak's nobles objected. Because of Perak's hostility, the Dutch withdrew from their garrison.

Dutch Ruthlessness

When the Dutch arrived in South East Asia, instead of merely buying spices they wanted to stop other countries from trading there. At first they did so peacefully making treaties with local rulers. But when the locals defied them, the Dutch used force. In 1621, in Lontor, when the locals refused to hand over all their nutmeg and mace, the Dutch attacked the island. Hundreds of islanders were sent into slavery, many killed, thousands died of starvation in the mountains rather than surrender. On Run, another island, all grown men were killed.

The Dutch controlled how much spice the inhabitants could grow. Because too much cloves were grown in Seram, the Dutch destroyed the clove trees so that hardly any cloves grew on the Maluku islands.

REBELLION AGAINST DUTCH POWER

Minangkabau Rebellion

In 1677 a Minangkabau prince, Raja Ibrahim led the states of Naning, Sungei Ujong and Rembau against the Dutch. With 4000 warriors, he managed to capture Dutch territory on the outskirts of Melaka. The Bugis in Kelang refused to support him and he was forced to retreat. He was later murdered. He is known to be the first ruler of Negri Sembilan.

A Near Uprising

In 1790 one of the largest Malay uprisings against the Dutch almost occurred. Malays from Trengganu, Rembau, Johor, Siak, Lingga and Siantan gathered 400 boats loaded with 8000 fighting men and a ground force of 20,000. European prisoners rowed these boats. With no single leader, the force soon split up and the Dutch were spared the attack.

Pulau Gotong Massacre

The Dutch had a fort at Pulau Gotong, a Sumatran island close to Johor. Raja Mohammad of Siak was the son of Raja Kechil once ruler of Riau-Johor. In 1759, he arrived with 40 vessels with gifts for the Dutch. After the Dutch received the sultan and his gifts, the sultan's men, armed with krises, killed the entire garrison. Two years later, the Dutch attacked Raja Mohammad. Although the Sultan used floating forts and fire ships that stretched the whole breath of the river, he was defeated. The Dutch then made his brother, Raja Alam, the new sultan of Siak.

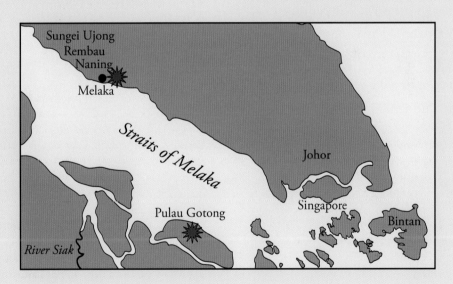

Find Out More

Melaka Empire
Riau-Johor
British Control

Early Kingdoms

The recorded history of the Malay peninsula began with several early kingdoms which existed between the 1st to the 5th centuries. Langkasuka, Kedah, Chi-tu and Kiu-li were mentioned is several Chinese historical records. Through archaeological excavations we can discover the exact locations of some of these lands. As maritime trade brought wealth, not surprisingly, these countries are found on rivers or have sea access.

The early kingdoms came about due to the important location of the Malay peninsula. The peninsula was strategically placed between the sea and land routes linking China and India. These port kingdoms also produced gold, tin, rainforest and sea products which they could use to trade.

As these lands had traded with India for centuries, they too followed the Indian religions. Hindu and Buddhist temples and artifacts have been found at several sites on the Malay peninsula.

"The King of Langkasuka and the nobles wear above their robes a red cloth ... They wear golden belts and bear gold rings to their ears. Women bear also scarves adorned with jewels ... When the King leaves the palace, he sits on an elephant under white umbrellas. He is preceded by drums and surrounded by fierce soldiers."

Liangshu
Chinese historical document

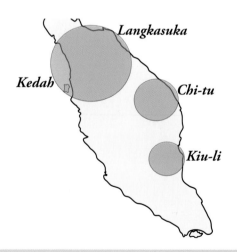

Find Out More

Srivijaya Empire
Indians
Living Stones and Cist Graves

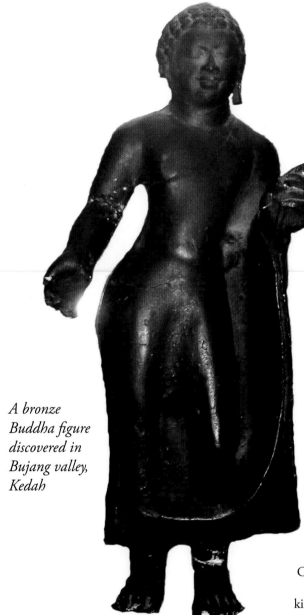

Langkasuka

According to Chinese historical documents, a city called Langkasuka was founded in the 2nd century. This city was located south of Patani in southern Thailand and extensive earthworks, moats and canals have been found there. In the year 515 Langkasuka's king, Bhagadatta, sent its first embassy to China. In the 7th century Langkasuka became part of the Srivijaya empire.

Kedah

In the vicinity of Langkasuka, but on its west coast, lay Kedah. Famous for producing tin and a wealthy trading centre, the country had also been called Kalah, Kadaram and Kataha. Temple sites have been found in the Bujang Valley and bronze, terracotta and stone artefacts have been unearthed there. These artefacts date from the 6th and 7th centuries and are Mahayana Buddhist artefacts. Mahayana Buddhism was the religion followed at that time. Like Langkasuka, the kingdom became part of the Srivijaya empire in the 7th century. Kedah became powerful again when Srivijaya went into decline.

A bronze Buddha figure discovered in Bujang valley, Kedah

Chit-tu

Chi-tu which means "red earth land" had been described in Chinese historical records. The kingdom was probably located in Kelantan and produced gold from its rivers.

Kiu-li

Another kingdom mentioned in the historical records is Kiu-li and may also have been called Koli. It is likely to have been located in Pahang. The country may have traded with the kingdom of Funan, which is located in present day South Vietnam.

An earthenware pot discovered in Kedah

Economy

In its early years, Malaysia was lucky as it had agricultural and mining products to export.

Despite the problems it caused in the tin mining states, tin brought great wealth in the 19th century. Rubber too became a main export due to its massive demand in the early 20th century. Later, palm oil became an export earner. In Borneo, wealth came from timber.

In the late 20th century, oil and gas overtook rubber exports and became hugely successful for Malaysia. This was also a time of great economic growth.

However, in the last thirty years, Malaysia no longer relied on agriculture and mining . It had become a strong manufacturing nation with a focus on computers and consumer electronics.

Tourism too became another main source of income.

"Europeans in Malaya ... are engaged [in] the rubber industry, tin mining, the legal and medical professions, commerce, and the public service, commerce being the predominating occupation in the Straits Settlements and the rubber industry in the Malay States."

Handbook to British Malaya (1927)

H.N. Ridley (left) was so keen on the rubber tree that he became known as "Mad" Ridley.

Wet-Rice Farming

As Malaya's population grew, the British encouraged the Malays to grow more rice. Areas of wet-rice or *padi* farming expanded in the north and northeast. However, the British still favoured other export crops. This meant that not many loans were made to *padi* farmers and not much money put into research.

Rubber

Seeds from the Rubber tree from Brazil first arrived in the Malay peninsula in 1877. A Director of the Botanical Gardens in Singapore, H.N.Ridley, experimented with the rubber tree and persuaded some planters to grow it. When rubber prices went up and coffee prices fell, many plantation owners planted the rubber tree and the government set aside land for the crop. By 1908 more rubber trees were planted than anything else. During the Emergency, planters faced grave difficulties. Today, Malaysia is one of the world's largest rubber producers.

Tin

For centuries Malays have collected tin by panning for the deposits in the streams. From the end of the 18th century, Chinese businessmen from the Straits Settlements took over the industry and opened large scale tin mines in Perak, Selangor and Linggi. Between 1870 and 1930, there was a huge demand for tin and prices shot up. When prices fell, however, tin mining became less attractive.

The Petronas twin towers was built on the wealth from oil and gas. Completed in 1998, it was once the tallest building in the world.

Malaysia Airlines

Malaysia Airlines began in 1947 with a flight from Singapore to Kuala Lumpur. The plane sat five. The airlines was then called Malayan Airways Limited.

When the Federation of Malaysia was formed in 1963, the airlines was known as Malaysian Airways Limited. After Singapore left Malaysia two years later, the name was changed to Malaysian-Singapore Airlines.

In 1972 this shared airlines was split into Singapore Airlines and Malaysian Airline System. Today, Malaysia Airlines has more than 100 aircraft servicing more than a hundred destinations.

In 1996, Malaysia Airlines faced new competition. A low cost airline called AirAsia, based in Kuala Lumpur, had taken off.

Palm Oil

The oil palm is a native of West Africa. It produces palm oil which is used in soap, candles, vegetable oils, margarine, grease and fuel for engines. The tree was introduced in the Malaya peninsula in the 1850s but only became a strong export commodity a hundred years later. Malaysia is the largest exporter and producer of palm oil.

An Oil Palm plantation

Oil and Gas

Because of the massive increase in the oil prices in the 1970s, many companies explored for oil in South East Asia. Offshore oil was found in Sabah, Sarawak and Terengganu. Oil has been described as "black gold". By 1980 earnings from oil exports well overtook earnings from rubber.

Malaysia is also one of the world's largest exporter of Liquified natural gas (LNG).

Find Out More

British Control
Tin Mine Wars
Emergency

New Economic Policy

After the May 13 riots, the government realised that poverty was one of the reasons for the ethnic violence. The rural Malays and Orang Asli were then the poorest ethnic groups in the country. The government wanted the economy to grow and it wanted to help the poor Malays. It set up public businesses to do this. In 1971, the New Economic Policy was launched. This economic campaign was taken over my the New Development Policy and later the National Vision Policy.

Tun Mahathir Mohamad was Malaysia's Prime Minister for 22 years. During that time, Malaysia's economy grew tremendously.

Manufacturing

Between 1970 and 1990 manufacturing grew strongly. With government encouragement, there were large investments in factories by foreign companies. Producing a wide range of goods from computers to air conditioners, from mobile phones to microwave ovens, manufacturing is Malaysia's top export earner.

Dato' Seri Abdullah Ahmad Badawi became Malaysia's Prime Minister in 2003.

Information Technology

Malaysia wants global information technology (IT) companies to invest in Malaysia. It also wants IT companies to do its research and development in Malaysia. To do this it created a zone called the Multimedia Super Corridor in the Klang Valley. It hopes to attract IT companies by providing high speed internet, attractive tax breaks and IT friendly laws. The zone is also close to the international airport and the seat of government in Putra Jaya. Global companies may open their offices at a specially created city called Cyberjaya.

Dato' Seri Najib Tun Razak, son of the 2nd Prime Minister, is to takeover as Prime Minister in 2009.

Key Dates

1900 - Malaya becomes the world's largest tin producer

1914 - Malaya is the world's largest rubber producer

1995 - Multimedia Super Corridor

2005 - Malaysia's economy since 1980 had gown by 10 times in size

Emergency

When the Second World War ended, the British returned to Malaya but the Communists wanted to turn Malaya into a communist country.

So the Communists began an armed struggle. Attacking rubber plantations and tin mines, they devastated Malaya's economy. Roads and railways were unsafe. More than a hundred British and Malayan civilians were being killed every month.

The British recruited more police and brought in troops from Britain, Australia, New Zealand, Fiji and Africa. The British also created "new villages" to isolate the Communists from their supporters.

This meant that the terrorists could no longer mount major attacks and were driven deep into the jungle. The Communists lost even more support when Malaya became independent.

"As soon as news of the attack reached [us, we] forced marched to the village ... The scene was horrible; a burning police station, dead policemen everywhere, women and children who had survived were wailing and crying."

Dato' J.J Raj (Jnr)
Smashing Terrorism in the Malayan Emergency by Brian Stewart

A Communist terrorist's cap with the five pointed red star, the symbol of communism.

British soldier and armoured car

From Heroes to Terrorists

During the Second World War, the Communists and the British were united because their common enemy was the Japanese. From hideouts in the jungle, the Communists, known as the Malayan People's Anti-Japanese Army (MPAJA), waged war against the Japanese occupiers. To help the Communists, the British sent them weapons.

When war ended, the MPAJA were regarded as heroes. But during the Emergency, the MPAJA used these same weapons to attack the British and, later, the Malayan government. The heroes had become Communist Terrorists.

Chin Peng

The Communists

Politics in the Chinese community in Malaya was similar to politics in China. Some people supported the Communists whilst others supported the Nationalist. Before the war, the Communists were active and well-organised in Malaya. Communism appealed to the poor Chinese, many of whom were squatters living on the fringe of the jungle. The Communists were mainly from the Chinese community although there were also a few from other races.

A British Spy

General Lai Tek, the Communist leader, was actually a British spy. He had often switched sides and once spied for the Japanese. In 1947, he fled the country with the party's funds. Chin Peng became the new Communist leader.

Casualties of the Emergency

	Police	Military	Civilians	Communists
Killed	1346	519	2,473	6,710
Wounded	1601	959	1,385	2,819

Source: Looking Back. Tunku Abdul Rahman

Sir Henry Gurney's car.
The red circles show bullet holes.

Memorial listing three periods of conflict: the Great War, the Second World War and, lastly, the Emergency

Assassination

In 1951, the Communists ambushed Sir Henry Gurney on the road to Fraser's Hill. He was the British High Commissioner, the highest ranking British official in Malaya. His car was riddled with bullet holes killing both Sir Henry and his driver. This was a blow to the British and Malayans.

Sir Henry was replaced by Sir Gerald Templer, an able man who helped defeat the Communists.

Find Out More

Second World War
Independence
Malaysia and Confrontation

New Villages

During the Emergency, half a million Chinese squatters who lived on the jungle fringe were moved by the government to "new villages". Many of these squatters were Communists supporters. They either believed in what the Communists promised or were forced by the Communists to support them.

These new villages were defended by Malayan forces and so the squatters were protected from terrorist threats. At the same time, Communist sympathisers were stopped from supplying the terrorists with food, medicine, weapons and recruits. The British gave the squatters modern utilities like electricity, running water and sewage and so many squatters stopped supporting the terrorists.

Propaganda leaflets showing a hungry terrorist who listens to rumours

Propaganda

The government distributed millions of leaflets to the population. Their aim was to persuade the locals to stop supporting the Communists and to encourage the terrorists to leave the organisation. Films shows were held around the country, ex-terrorists gave speeches and the national radio was used to spread the message.

Book of Communists teachings used by the MPAJA

End of the Emergency

In the 1950s, many new political parties were formed. These catered to the population's interests. They criticised the British, demanded citizenship and called for independence. When Malaya became independent in 1957, the Communists were left without a real cause to fight for.

Key Dates

1948 - Start of the Emergency

1951 - Sir Henry Gurney is assassinated

1955 - Tunku Abdul Rahman meets Communists leader, Chin Peng, in Baling for peace talks

1960 - End of the Emergency

Independence

The Malayan flag had 11 stripes and an 11-pointed star, one for each state.

After the Second World War, the Philippines, India, Pakistan, Burma and Indonesia became independent. Soon it would be Malaya's turn. Granting Malaya its independence would not be easy though. The Chinese and Indian migrants wanted to become citizens of the new country; whilst the indigenous Malays wanted to safeguard their Malay rights. Malaya would only be independent when its races were united.

The Alliance was a coalition which united the Malays, Chinese and Indian political parties. They agreed to a constitution. This document gave Malays political domination and special rights. It also allowed the other races to become citizens, to have a role in politics and have a right to practice their cultures. With the various races so united, Britain granted Malaya its independence.

"... the clock in the tower began to strike: the [flags] began to move ... the Union Jack downwards, the Federation Flag upwards. As the last stroke of midnight resonated ... a band played 'God Save the Queen' followed by 'Negara-ku'."

Mubin Sheppard
Tunku His Life & Times

Onn Ja'afar was UMNO's founder and first leader (1946-1951). After leaving UMNO, he founded the Independence of Malaya party and, later, Parti Negara.

At a ceremony on August 31st, Tunku Abdul Rahman, Malaya's first Prime Minister, declared the country's independence (merdeka).

Malayan Union

After the Second World War, the British wanted to join the Malay states into, what it called, a 'Malayan Union'. With this plan, the Malay rulers would no longer be heads of their own states and the new monarch of Malaya would be the British King.

The Malays opposed the Union because there would lose their Malay rights and the Malay rulers would lose their status. A large number of migrants would also become Malayan citizens. The Malays feared they would be outnumbered. Because of this Malay opposition, the British gave up their idea and replaced it with a new one: the Federation of Malaya.

UMNO logo

UMNO

To oppose the Malayan Union, Onn Ja'afar and other Malays formed a political party called United Malays National Organisation (UMNO). They held public demonstrations against the Malayan Union. Onn Ja'afar wanted other races to be able to join UMNO too. The other members did not agree and Onn Ja'afar left to form his own political party. Tunku Abdul Rahman replaced him as the party's new leader.

Key Dates

1946 - Malayan Union proposed

1946 - Formation of UMNO

1953 - Formation of Alliance

1957 - Malaya becomes independent

ALLIANCE LEADERS

From left: Tunku Abdul Rahman (UMNO leader and Prime Minister 1957-1970), Tan Siew Sin (MCA leader) and V.T Sambanthan (MIC leader)

The Alliance

The Malayan Chinese Association (MCA) started as a social welfare organisation for the Chinese community. It became a political party in 1952. The Malayan Indian Congress (MIC), which represented the Indian community, was formed in 1946. After Onn Ja'afar resigned from UMNO, Tunku Abdul Rahman became UMNO's president. To unite the three races and to fight for independence, he formed a coalition between UMNO, MCA and MIC which was called the Alliance.

The Alliance logo

In 1971 the Alliance included many more political parties. The coalition was called National Front or Barisan Nasional. Its logo is above.

The Constitution

Each race was worried about what would happen once the British left. Would the Malays or the migrant races dominate? Fortunately and skillfully the Alliance leaders came to a compromise on the rights of each community. This agreement was written into the Constitution. The Constitution is a law above all other laws.

The Malays would have special rights, political power, Malay as the official language and Islam as the official religion

The Chinese and Indians would have citizenship, the right to practise their culture and religion, Chinese and Tamil schools to continue

Rights of each community within the Constitution

The Agong

Malaya had nine sultans with each ruling a different state, but there was no single ruler for the entire country. When Malaya became independent, a unique form of kingship was created. Each ruler would take turns to become king. After five years, they would choose one amongst their number as the new monarch. The king was called the Yang DiPertuan Agong or 'Paramount Ruler'. The first Agong was Tuanku Abdul Rahman of Negri Sembilan. It is a unique system that has worked successfully to this day.

Tun Abdul Razak became the Deputy Prime Minister at the time of independence. He was Prime Minister from 1970-1976.

Tuanku Abdul Rahman (first Yang Dipertuan Agong) stands between Tunku Abdul Rahman Putra, first Prime Minister (left) and Donald MacGillivray, last British High Commissioner (right)

May 13 Riots

Twelve years after Malaya's independence, racial riots erupted in Kuala Lumpur. The 1969 election campaign was emotional with each race questioning their place in the new country. Language and education were big issues. As the Alliance faired poorly, the opposition political parties held marches to celebrate. UMNO countered with its own rally. Racial violence then broke out. The government declared a state of emergency. The bloody fighting lasted for four days.

Ja'afar Onn's son, Tun Hussein Onn, rejoined UMNO and later became the country's third Prime Minister. He was Prime Minister from 1976 to 1981.

Find Out More

British Control
Second World War
Malaysia and Confrontation

Indians

For over a thousand years people from India had visited the Malay peninsula which they called "the Land of Gold". We know from old temples sites that they arrived in the 3rd century or earlier. The Malays adopted Indian culture including their writing, stories, kingship and the Hindu religion.

In the 13th century, Gujeratis from India's west coast and the Chettiars from Tamilnad sailed to the Malay peninsula to trade. Many were Muslims and so spread Islam to the Malays.

During the British colonial period, Indians migrated to Malaya to work as labourers in British plantations. They worked on rubber, sugar and coffee plantations and, later, on the railways. Conditions in the plantations were poor with many workers getting sick and many fled these plantations.

Many Indians also worked as moneylenders, accountants, financiers, surveyors, engineers and lawyers. Many sikhs joined the police force.

Population Growth

In the year 2000, the number of Indians in Malaysia was around two million, which was 9% of the country's population. The table below shows the population growth:

Year	Population	As a % of Malaya's population
1871	33,390	11%
1911	267,170	10%
1931	621,847	14%
1957	735,038	10%

Source: Guy Hunter. South East Asia: Race, Culture, Nation

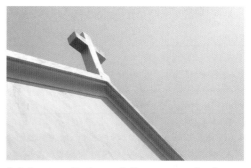

Malaysian Indians follow many faiths including Hinduism, Islam and Christianity

Find Out More

Srivijaya Empire
Early Kingdoms
Chinese

*Indian culture had spread to much of the
Malay archipelago. This carving is from Java.*

Indian Community

Although called 'Indians', the migrants from
the Indian subcontinent included Tamil,
Telegu, Malayali, Sikhs, Punjabis,
Pathans, Ceylon Tamils,
Ceylonese and Pakistanis. They
were grouped together but
community each had its own
language, religion and culture.
Most of the Indians that came
to the Malay peninsula were
Tamil, Telegu or Malayali. In
terms of size, the next group
were the Sikhs, Punjabis or
Pathans. This was followed by
the Ceylon Tamils, Ceylonese
and Pakistanis. Although
some Indians in Malaysia are
Christians or Muslims, most are
Hindus or Sikhs.

A Hindu god

Thamboosamy Pillai

Thamboosamy Pillai migrated from India
in 1875. He worked as a Treasury Clerk for
the British Resident in Selangor and later
went into business. One of his
business partners was the Chinese
entrepreneur, Loke Yew.
Thamboosamy Pillai's ventures
were very successful and in 1889
built the Hindu temple, Sri Maha
Mariamman in Kuala Lumpur.

He is but one
example of a poor
Indian migrant
becoming rich and
successful.

Thamboosamy Pillai

Living Stones and Cist Graves

Megaliths are mainly found in Negri Sembilan, Melaka, Sarawak's Kelabit Highlands and the coastal plains of Sabah. These are large rocks which have been placed upright and may have been used as monuments, shrines or grave sites.

In Negri Sembilan and Melaka, the megaliths are often seen in groups or "avenues". Locals call them "living stones" or "batu hidup" because some believe they grow with time. The most famous stones are those at Pengkalan Kempas. The exact age of the stones are unknown but it is likely that they pre-date the arrival of Islam.

Cist graves or slab graves are coffins made of stone. Dating from the Iron Age, the most recent graves are from the 1st to 7th centuries. Related to cist graves, dolmens are flat rocks placed on tombs. Dolmens are mainly found in Sabah and Sarawak.

"...we may suggest that the most likely period when these stones were erected is: between AD 1000 and 1500. Thus they would be related not to the prehistory period, but rather to the classical era of Southeast Asian history ..."

John N. Miksic
"From Seri Vijaya to Melaka Batu Tagak in Historical and Cultural Context" JMBRAS Vol. LX Part 2 1987

Living Stones at Pengkalan Kempas, Negri Sembilan. From left: 'The Rudder', 'The Spoon' and 'The Sword'

Find Out More

Prehistory
Early Kingdoms
Minangkabaus

*A cist grave
discovered in
Perak*

Cist Graves

Cist graves have been found in southern Perak
and northern Selangor. Granite slabs are used
to create the coffin. Many objects have been
found in the graves including pottery, tools,
precious stones, spearheads and ornaments.
The people of the time may have thought
that these items would be used by the dead
person in the next world. Cist graves were
likely reserved for people of high status in the
community.

Living Stones

We do not know whether these megaliths
were just monuments or had other uses.
Some living stones may have been used
as grave sites. Others may have been back
rests for a ruler or chief to use during
meetings. They may have had a function
during rituals, like tying a water buffalo
to it before slaughter. Many megaliths
have also been found in West Sumatra
which suggests some connection to
Minangkabau culture.

The Ordeal Stone

Sword, Spoon and Rudder

Because of their shapes, the stones at
Pengkalan Kempas are known as The
Sword, The Spoon and The Rudder. Unlike
other megaliths, they are elaborately carved.
They may be of Hindu origin but one of
the stones has the word 'Allah' inscribed
on it. Beside the stones, lies the tomb of
Sheikh Ahmad Majnun who died in 1467.
Curiously, one inscription says that he was
a saint whilst another says he was a traitor.

Next to the tomb is the "ordeal stone".
Legend says that if you tell a lie with you
hand in the hole, the stone will tighten
around it painfully.

Malaysia and Confrontation

After Malaya's independence, its Prime Minister, Tunku Abdul Rahman, suggested that North Borneo, Sarawak, Brunei and Singapore join Malaya to form a new country. Singapore already had its own self government whilst the other territories were ruled by the British.

Most North Borneons and Sarawakians wanted to join Malaya. Singapore's Prime Minister, Lee Kwan Yew, was also keen. So a new country was born on 16 September 1963. It was called the Federation of Malaysia. Because of political problems, Singapore was expelled from the federation two years later.

The Phillipines and Indonesia opposed the formation of Malaysia. Indonesia took up arms in a conflict called "The Confrontation".

"The word 'Malaysia' has been used since the nineteenth century ... to include all the islands from the north-western tip of Sumatra across to the easternmost Spice Islands ... [In] 1961 the name was revived ... it consists of but a small corner of the Malaysia referred to in the past."

Wang Gungwu
Malaysia: A Survey

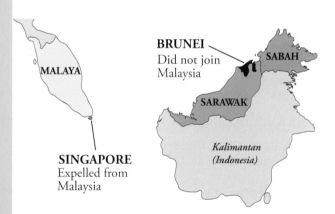

BRUNEI
Did not join Malaya

MALAYA

SABAH

SARAWAK

Kalimantan (Indonesia)

SINGAPORE
Expelled from Malaysia

Key Dates

1963 - Formation of Malaysia

1963 - Confrontation with Indonesia

1965 - Singapore leaves Malaysia

1966 - Confrontation ends

There was heavy fighting along the Sabah and Sarawak borders with Indonesia. The Confrontation almost became a full-scale war.

Philippines's Opposition

The Philippines claimed Sabah as part of their country. Sabah once belonged to the Sultante of Sulu which was in the Philippines. So the country opposed the formation of Malaysia. This problem was later solved through discussions. In 1966, the Philippines recognised Malaysia as a country.

Indonesian Confrontation

President Sukarno of Indonesia wanted Sabah and Sarawak to be part of his country. He wanted a 'Greater Indonesia' which would include Sabah, Sarawak and perhaps even Malaya. From Borneo, Indonesian soldiers attacked Sabah and Sarawak. Troops from Britain, Australia and New Zealand came to Malaysia's aid and stopped the Indonesian attacks. Indonesia dropped bombs on Singapore. It also parachuted troops into Johor but these attackers were quickly caught. This Confrontation ended when President Sukarno was ousted as Indonesia's President.

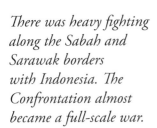

The Malaysian flag has 14 stripes and a 14-pointed star. Each represents a state with the 14th representing the federal government.

A bronze figure from the National Monument, Tugu Negara

Brunei

Brunei was supposed to join the Federation of Malaya but its leaders changed their minds. They preferred not to share Brunei's wealth from oil. Huge oil reserves had been discovered there. Another reason was that the Sultan of Brunei did not want to wait his turn before becoming the Agong. Malaya's rulers could not agree to this. Brunei did not join Malaysia and only became an independent country in 1984.

Find Out More

Borneo
Singapore
Independence

Melaka Empire

Ships sailing to the Spice Islands to trade had to pass through the Melaka Straits. At its narrowest point lay Melaka which taxed these ships and so the kingdom became wealthy.

As more ships stopped at the kingdom, soon Melaka itself became a trading destination. Different wares were bought and sold there including spice from the Spice Islands, silks from China, camphor from Borneo and cotton cloth from India.

Melaka's navy were Sea Gypsies who kept its waters free from pirates. The kingdom was also protected by its overlord, China, and became an empire. When the people of Melaka converted to Islam, it gave the empire greater prestige. Muslim traders preferred to deal with a Muslim trading centre and Melaka's wealth grew.

The Malays ruled here for over a hundred years. This came to an end when the Portuguese invaded Melaka in 1511.

Melaka's Government

Sultan

Bendahara
Chief Minister

Temenggong
Chief of Police

Laksamana
Admiral

Penghulu Bendahari
Treasurer

Shah Bandar *Chinese Leader* **Shah Bandar** *Gujerat Leader* **Shah Bandar** *Tamil Leader* **Shah Bandar** *Arab Leader*

Although the Sultan was the head of government, the Bendahara was very powerful and ran the day to day affairs.

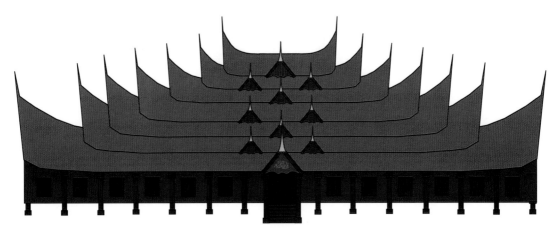

Sultan Mansur Shah's palace, built around 1460

> *"Melaka became famous as a very great city ... so much so that princes from all countries came to present themselves before [the] sultan ... who [bestowed] upon them robes of honour ... and rich presents of jewels, gold and silver."*

Sejarah Melayu
(Malay Annals)

A Malay warrior. Similar clothes may have been worn during the time of the Melaka Empire.

A Famous Bendahara

Tun Perak was Melaka's most famous Bendahara and served under four different Sultans. During his forty-two years as Chief Minister, Melaka became an empire and most of the Malay peninsula including the east coast of Sumatra came under Melaka's control. During Tun Perak's time and the reign of Sultan Muzaffar Shah, Melaka beat off several Siamese attacks.

Naming of Melaka

One day Prince Paramesvara went hunting when his dog chased a mousedeer. Instead of fleeing, the mousedeer turned and kicked the dog. Paramesvara was impressed that the mousedeer was full of fight. This was a good sign and he decided that he and his followers should live here. As he was standing beneath a Melaka tree, he called this place 'Melaka'.

Introduction of Islam

In the early 15th century, Islam became Melaka's main religion when its ruler converted to Islam. This brought greater prestige to Melaka for in Muslim ideas of kingship the ruler was "God's shadow on earth".

Islam had arrived in the region much earlier. The kingdom of Pasai in Sumatra had converted to Islam in the 1250s. The earliest evidence of Islam on the Malay peninsula is found on a granite block called the Terengganu Stone. Containing Islamic inscriptions the stone is dated 1303. In East Malaysia, the earliest evidence is a Muslim woman's gravestone in Brunei dated 1048. It is likely that traders from Gujerat in India first introduced Islam to the Malay archipelago.

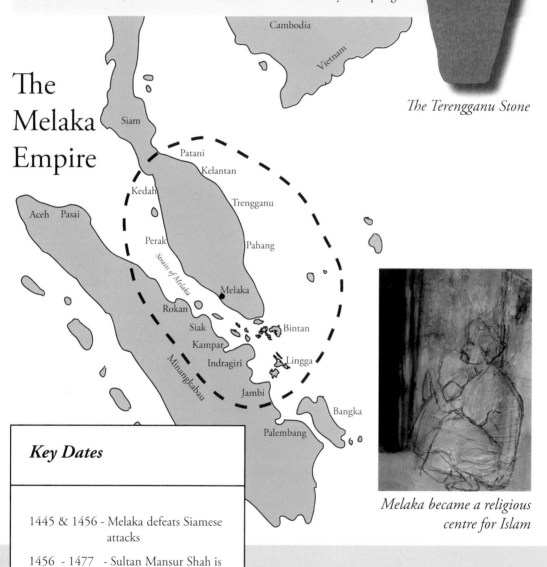

The Terengganu Stone

The Melaka Empire

Cambodia

Vietnam

Siam

Patani

Kelantan

Kedah

Trengganu

Aceh Pasai

Perak

Pahang

Straits of Melaka

Melaka

Rokan

Siak Bintan

Kampar

Indragiri Lingga

Minangkabau

Jambi

Bangka

Palembang

Melaka became a religious centre for Islam

Key Dates

1445 & 1456 - Melaka defeats Siamese attacks

1456 - 1477 - Sultan Mansur Shah is ruler

1456 - 1498 - Tun Perak is Bendahara

Islam and the Malay language

Melaka converted to Islam in the early 15th century. As Muslim Indian traders preferred to do business with fellow Muslims, they now traded in Melaka too. This made Melaka even richer. Melaka became a centre for Islam and helped spread the religion throughout the Malay world. Likewise, Melaka also helped spread the Malay language as a common language for trading.

Spice Islands

The Spice Islands were the islands of the Moluccas. These islands grew cloves, nutmegs, mace and other spices which were greatly traded and made Melaka rich. It was the search for the Spice Islands that led to Europe's great voyages of exploration in the 16th Century. After capturing Melaka in 1511, the Portuguese were the first Europeans to arrive at the Spice Islands. Today these islands are known as the Maluku islands and are in Indonesia.

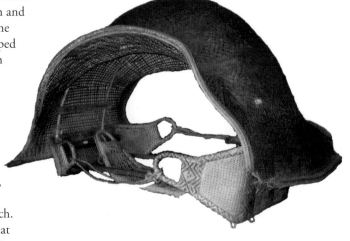

Unlike the simple howdah shown above, the Sultan's howdah was richly decorated in gold. A howdah is a seat with a canopy used for riding on top of an elephant.

The Story of Hang Tuah

Hang Tuah was a great warrior and very popular with the people. The Sultan became jealous. Accusing Hang Tuah of committing treason, he ordered his Bendahara to kill the warrior.

Hang Tuah was very loyal to his Ruler and said he was willing to die if the Sultan commanded it. The Bendahara, knowing this was an injustice, pretended to follow the Ruler's orders but instead of killing Hang Tuah, he asked him to hide in the jungle.

When Hang Tuah's best friend, Hang Jebat, learnt that Hang Tuah had been killed, he became furious. Using Hang Tuah's magic kris, he attacked the palace and killed many people. The Sultan then said that he wished Hang Tuah was still alive. Hearing this, the Bendahara brought Hang Tuah out of hiding and the Ruler commanded him to kill Hang Jebat.

Hang Tuah and Hang Jebat fought for hours until, finally, Hang Tuah grabbed the magic kris and killed Hang Jebat.

Find Out More

Paramesvara
Portuguese Invasion
Riau-Johor

Minangkabaus

From the 15th century, the Minangkabaus migrated from West Sumatra to the Malay peninsula. As the Minangkabaus were agricultural people, they did not settle on the coast but instead made their homes in the interior.

Eventually there were nine groups of Minangkabau villages and so the area was called Negri Sembilan or 'The Nine States'.

Each state has its own ruling chief. The chiefs of Sungai Ujong, Rembau, Jelebu and Johol were the most powerful and used the title 'Undang' (which means 'Lawgiver'). They had a right to choose a successor to the ruler. The ruler's main function was to unite Negri Sembilan.

As in Perak and Selangor, there were also disputes over tin. This led the British to take control of Sungai Ujong. Eventually, all of Negri Sembilan was controlled by a single British Resident.

> *"... land might only belong to women ... Every man lived on his wife's land or on his mother's or sister's land ... every man had, sooner or later, to leave his own village and settle in the village of his wife."*

Dr Nellie S.L. Tan-Wong
Adat Perpatih

Adat Perpatih

The Minangkabaus followed the 'adat perpatih' or matrilinial traditions. This is where where inheritance and socio-economic power follows the female line. It is one of the few cultures in the world that practises this system.

Istana Lama or the 'Old Palace' in Seri Menanti. Not a single nail was used in its construction.

The 7th Yang DiPertuan Besar, Tuanku Muhammad, with bodyguards

Map of Negri Sembilan, showing each of its nine states.

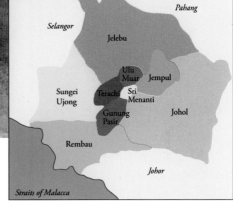

Key Dates

1677 - Raja Ibrahim from West Sumatra becomes ruler of Negri Sembilan

1830 - Raja Radin becomes first locally born ruler of the state

1874 - Sungei Ujong accepts a British Resident

1895 - Negri Sembilan is unified under a single British Resident

The Nine States

The nine Minangkabau states on the Malay peninsula were called 'Negri Sembilan' which means 'The Nine States' or 'The Nine Counties'. Over the course of history, parts of the Nine States have been absorbed by Selangor, Melaka, Pahang and Johor. This reduced Negri Sembilan's size to the territory as shown above. Today, Negri Sembilan is unique because it is a federation within the Federation of Malaysia.

Statue of Adityawarman

Founder of Minangkabau

Around 1347 Adityawarman founded the Minangkabau kingdom in West Sumatra. At first, he ruled the kingdom of Malayu, on the Sumatran coast, but later moved inland into the mountains of Minangkabau. Adityawarman was a Siwa-Buddhist, a religion practised by Javanese kings at the time. He left behind many inscriptions which are written in a combination of Sanskrit and Old Malay.

Yang DiPertuan Besar

The rulers of Negri Sembilan used the Minangkabau title 'Yang DiPertuan Besar' ('Him that is made Lord') which is shortened to 'Yamtuan'. This title was at times also used in other Malay states until the Arabic title of 'Sultan' became favoured. Today the title is only used in Negri Sembilan. The title 'Yang DiPertuan Agong' (which means 'Paramount Ruler') for Malaysia's king was taken from the Negri Sembilan title.

Minangkabau Princes

Raja Ibrahim, the first Minangkabau ruler of Negri Sembilan had launched attacks against Dutch Melaka. Almost fifty years after his death, the chiefs went to Minangkabau to ask its King to sent a prince to Negri Sembilan to become their ruler. So in 1721 Raja Melewar travelled to Negri Sembilan to become its ruler. The next two rulers were also Minangkabau princes. The first Yamtuan to be born in Negri Sembilan was Raja Radin. His son, Yamtuan Antah, fought against British rule but was defeated. The rulers of Negri Sembilan today are descendants of Raja Radin.

Yamtuan Antah in exile in Singapore

Negri Sembilan's Traditional Government

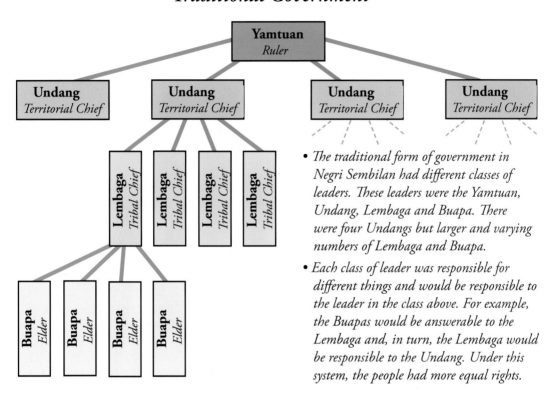

Yamtuan
Ruler

Undang
Territorial Chief

Undang
Territorial Chief

Undang
Territorial Chief

Undang
Territorial Chief

Lembaga
Tribal Chief

Lembaga
Tribal Chief

Lembaga
Tribal Chief

Lembaga
Tribal Chief

Buapa
Elder

Buapa
Elder

Buapa
Elder

Buapa
Elder

- *The traditional form of government in Negri Sembilan had different classes of leaders. These leaders were the Yamtuan, Undang, Lembaga and Buapa. There were four Undangs but larger and varying numbers of Lembaga and Buapa.*

- *Each class of leader was responsible for different things and would be responsible to the leader in the class above. For example, the Buapas would be answerable to the Lembaga and, in turn, the Lembaga would be responsible to the Undang. Under this system, the people had more equal rights.*

Origins of the "Minangkabau" name

Legend says that in ancient times a Javanese army invaded Minangkabau. Because neither side won the battle, the Javanese and Minangkabaus agreed that the outcome would be decided by a bull fight.

The Javanese chose a big, strong water buffalo. The Minangkabaus chose instead an unweaned calf which they separated from its mother until it was starving. Because the calf had no horns, the Minangkabaus tied knives to its head.

During the fight, the calf was so desperate to nurse that, when it faced the fierce bull, it frenziedly nuzzled the stronger animal's belly in search of a teat, stabbing the bigger animal to death. Because of this event, the locals took the name "Minangkabau" which means "The Victorious Water Buffalo".

Find Out More

Bugis
Dutch Influence
Rebellion Against British Rule

65

Orang Asli

The Orang Asli, which means "original peoples", are the indigenous inhabitants of the Malay peninsula. There are three main tribal groups: Semang (also known as "Negrito"), Senoi and Proto-Malay. Each group is made out of various sub-groups.

Generally, the Semangs are found in the north, the Senois in the middle of the peninsula and Proto-Malay are mainly to the south.

The Semang, who number about two thousand, are regarded as the earliest inhabitants of the Malay Peninsula. The Senois are the group with the largest Orang Asli population and they number about 30,000. The Senois and Proto-Malays arrived much later than the Semang. There are currently about 140,000 Orang Asli in Malaysia. Each group has its own language and culture.

A wooden statue of an Orang Asli spirit

"The gods were our creators and they once walked on Tanah Tujuh, which is the name of this world [for the Temuans]. Then ... the stairway was broken [and] the gods could only speak to us through dreams."

Antares
Tanah Tujuh

Find Out More

Living Stones and Cist Graves
Prehistory
Paramesvara

Ways of life

The Senois practise slash-and-burn farming. They slash the jungle, waiting for it to dry, then burning it. Crops are then planted. Because the land becomes infertile, the Senois have to move on, returning several years later. In contrast, the Semangs are hunter gatherers and live off the jungle's flora and fauna. They are constantly on the move. The Proto-Malays combine farming or fishing with collecting jungle or sea products to trade.

Orang Asli children

The new arrivals

When the Malays begun to arrive on the Malay peninsula, they recognised that the Orang Asli "owned" the land. Sometimes they intermarried with the Orang Asli which gave their descendants land rights. At other times, they paid the Orang Asli for taking over their lands. Unfortunately, the new arrivals also raided the Orang Asli to capture women and children. These captives became slaves. It is no surprise that the word "Semang" means slave.

Language

Generally, the Orang Asli's language has close links to the Austroasiatic languages; these are the languages of mainland Asia. In contrast, the Malay language is Austronesian, a family of languages spread amongst the islands of South East Asia. Through contact with these peoples, the language of the Proto-Malay have developed Austronesian features.

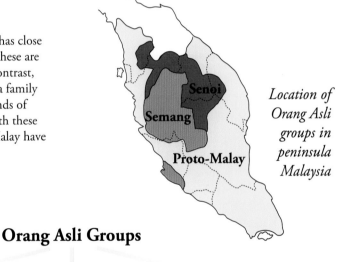

Location of Orang Asli groups in peninsula Malaysia

Orang Asli Groups

Semang	Senoi	Proto-Malay
Kensiu	Temiar	Temuan
Kintaq	Semai	Semelai
Lanoh	Semoq Beri	Jakun
Jahai	Jah Hut	Kanaq
Mandrik	Mah Meri	Kuala
Batek	Che Wong	Seletar

Pahang Civil War

Through the centuries, there have been many civil wars in the Malay kingdoms. Usually in war one kingdom invades another but in a civil war the two sides are from the same kingdom.

The Pahang Civil War lasted for five years and was fought between two brothers: Wan Mutahir and Wan Ahmad. When their father, Bendahara Ali, died, the younger Ahmad refused to recognise Mutahir as the new Bendahara.

Mutahir found support from Johor whilst Ahmad was supported by Trengganu, Kelantan and Rembau. Various parties were involved in the war including the British and the Siamese. Baginda Omar, Sultan Ali of Muar and Sultan Mahmud of Riau-Johor gave support to different sides.

Eventually, Ahmad successfully defeated his elder brother and became Bendahara of Pahang. Later, he became the kingdom's first sultan.

"... Mahmud Muzaffar Shah ex-Sultan ... [rightly] head of the royal house of Johor, Pahang and Lingga who deposed by the Dutch ... was now looking for a new throne."

R.O. Windstedt
A History of Johore

The Bendahara's Power

Pahang was still part of the kingdom of Riau-Johor. Because Britain and Holland had split the kingdom between themselves, Pahang could now act independently. Its Sultan, who was under Dutch control, had no power over his territories on the Malay peninsula; these were under British influence. This meant that the Bendahara in Pahang was all powerful. When Bendahara Ali passed away, his eldest son, Mutahir, became the Bendahara. His younger brother, Ahmad, disagreed and started a civil war.

A Sultan visits Siam

Sultan Mahmud of Riau-Johor had been deposed by the Dutch. When he heard of the troubles in Pahang, he visited the Siamese court and received support from the Siamese King. Sultan Mahmud took Ahmad's side and if Ahmad won, Ahmad would become the Bendahara. Sultan Mahmud hoped to then become the ruler of Pahang. The Siamese King supported the two men because once they had captured Pahang, that kingdom would be loyal to Siam.

Sultan Ahmad Shah, formerly known as Wan Ahmad.

Britain's Wrath

Supporting Wan Ahmad, Baginda Omar allowed Wan Ahmad and Sultan Mahmud into Trengganu with three Siamese ships. The merchants were worried that the Siamese would now attack Pahang. The British sent a warship and fired on the Kuala Trengganu fort killing twenty men. Not wanting to go to war with the British, the Siamese soon departed.

The New Bendahara

A year after the shelling of Trengganu, Wan Ahmad attacked Pahang. Mutahir and his son fled to Johor but died soon after. Without any rivals, Wan Ahmad then became Bendahara. Sultan Mahmud too later died.

Baginda Omar

Baginda Omar was no stranger to civil war. He was supposed to become Trengganu's new ruler but his uncle attacked him. Omar had to flee to the island of Lingga. Omar's uncle then became Sultan.

When the Sultan died, his young son became the new ruler. Omar returned and defeated the new sultan. Omar called himself Baginda Omar as 'Baginda' meant 'Conqueror'. Baginda Omar was a religious and wise ruler and Trengganu thrived under him.

Key Dates

1858 - Start of Pahang civil war

1861 - Wan Ahmad seeks support from Siam

1862 - British warship shell Kuala Trengganu

1863 - End of Pahang civil war

Find Out More

Riau-Johor
Tin Mine Wars
Siamese Invasion

69

Paramesvara

Prince Paramesvara (also spelled 'Parameswara') was the ruler of Palembang in Sumatra. His name meant "Supreme Person" and he was married to a Majapahit princess. Because he refused to obey the Mahapahit king, who was his overlord, they attacked him.

With his loyal Sea Gypsies, Paramesvara fled and sailed up the Riau-Lingga archipelago. He then travelled to Temasik, where he killed its chief, and became its ruler. After spending several years on Temasik, which he renamed Singapore, he was attacked again, this time by the Siamese. He fled to Muar on the Malay peninsula. Later, further north, he founded a new kingdom in a small village, called Melaka.

As his kingdom was threatened by attacks from Siam and Majapahit, Paramesvara obtained protection from China. Melaka became a wealthy trading centre and grew into an empire. It was ruled by Paramesvara and his descendants for a hundred years.

"… the raja enquiring the name of the tree under which he was standing, was informed that it was called the malaca tree. 'Then,' said he, 'let the name of the city be called Malaca'."

John Leyden's Malay Annals

Sea Gypsies with their house boat

Key Dates

~ 1400 - Paramesvara settles in Melaka

1409 - Admiral Cheng Ho visits Melaka

1411 - Paramesvara travels to China

1413 - Paramesvara dies

Three magical princes

Descendants of Srivijaya

Paramesvara was a descendant of the rulers of the once great Srivijaya empire. The empire was long gone but Paramesvara was ruler of Palembang in Sumatra which was once the capital of Srivijaya. Because of the legend of Seguntang Hill, his people saw him as a divine prince. His people were called Malays and took their name from the river Melayu which flowed in Sumatra. The Malays followed the traditions and customs of Srivijaya. Many of these traditions are still practised today.

Sea Gypsies

The Sea Gypsies or "Orang Selat" were indigenous people of the riverine and seas. They were very loyal to Paramesvara and to the rulers of Srivijaya. They lived on boats and fished for food. The Portuguese called them "Celates". They knew the seas and mangroves very well and became Paramesvara's navy.

Friend of China

When ships from China under Admiral Cheng Ho (also know as Zheng He) visited Melaka, Paramesvara agreed to become China's vassal and married a Chinese princess, Hang Li Po. Together with Cheng Ho, Paramesvara visited his new overlord, the Emperor of China. Under China's protection, Melaka flourished and became rich.

A Chinese junk

Legend of Seguntang Hill

Two women plant some rice padi on the green slopes of Seguntang Hill. At night they see a strange light there. In the morning they find that the padi had golden grains and leaves of silver. Then three princes, descendants of Alexandar the Great, come down the hill. The eldest prince is mounted on a water buffalo whilst one of his brothers holds a sword and the other grasps a spear. The chief of Palembang, Demang Lebar Daun, pays homage to these magical princes. Kings from all around visit them, bearing gifts. The eldest prince then becomes king of Minangkabau, the middle prince becomes king of Tanjung Pura and the youngest prince, called Sri Tri Buana ('Lord of the Three Worlds') becomes king of Palembang.

Find Out More

Singapore
Melaka Empire
Srivijaya Empire

Penang

Francis Light persuaded the Kedah sultan to lease Penang ("Betel-nut island") to the East India Company. When the Sultan died, his son, Sultan Abdullah, carried out his father's wishes. Francis Light then landed on Penang with three ships and a small garrison of troops. He re-named it the 'Prince of Wales Island'.

In exchange for Penang, the British promised to send troops to protect Kedah from its enemies. This promise could not be kept as the British government forbade the East India Company from fighting any wars.

Feeling betrayed, Sultan Abdullah, with 200 ships, tried to re-take the island but was defeated. With little choice, he transferred Penang to the British for 6000 Spanish dollars a year. The British built George Town and Penang became a freeport.

Together with Melaka and Singapore, Penang became part of the Straits Settlements, which were British colonies in Malaya.

"To hasten the chopping of wood on Penang, Francis Light loaded a cannon with a bag of silver dollars and shot it into the jungle."

A British ship

Why Penang?

For centuries the island of Penang belonged to Kedah. With the increase in trade and wealth, the British were looking for a trading base in South East Asia. They also no longer wanted to be dependent on Dutch ports of Batavia (today called "Jakarta") and Melaka.

The British managed to take control of Penang because the Kedah Sultan needed British help. The British now had their first foothold in the Melaka Straits.

Find Out More

Siamese Invasion
British Control
Singapore

Statue of Sir Francis Light. He died in 1794 and is buried in Penang.

The Kedah Sultan

Sultan Muhammad Jiwa fought his brother in a civil war. The Selangor Bugis, after helping the Sultan defeat his brother, then demanded large rewards. As the Sultan could not afford to pay the Bugis, they invaded Kedah and he fled north, where he met Francis Light. In exchange for Penang, the young captain promised to send British troops to protect Kedah's enemies: the Siamese to the north and the Bugis to the south.

Map of Penang

Province Wellesley

Sultan Abdullah was unable to re-take Penang by force. He later agreed to transfer a strip of mainland to the British for a payment of 10,000 Spanish dollars a year. This strip of land, which the Malays called Prai, was more than twice the size of Penang. Renaming it Province Wellesley, the British now had complete control of the channel and a better source of food supplies.

East India Company

The British East India Company was given permission by the British government to trade in the Far East. The company had its own police, army and courts to govern the territories it controlled, including Penang. Existing for 260 years, the British East India company was abolished in 1858.

Key Dates

1771 - Francis Light first meets Sultan Muhammad Jiwa

1786 - Francis Light starts a British settlement in Penang

1791 - Sultan Abdullah tries to retake Penang

1800 - The British obtain Province Wellesley

Portuguese Invasion

The Portuguese wanted to control the spice trade. To take charge of the sea routes in Asia they needed naval fortresses.

Melaka was wealthy, powerful and a trading centre en route to the spice islands. The Portuguese eyed Melaka and sent Diogo Lopes de Sequeira there with five ships. At first the Melakans traded with the Portuguese but many locals did not welcome the Portuguese competition. One night, the Melakans attacked, captured two Portuguese ships and set them alight. But Sequeira escaped.

To avenge this attack, Alfonso de Albuqueque arrived in Melaka with eighteen ships and a thousand men. Although outnumbered, the Portuguese were better armed and led by an experienced commander. The Melakans were disunited and many refused to fight . The Portuguese captured the city and the Sultan and his followers fled into the interior.

"The Portuguese fired their cannon from their ships so that the cannon balls came like rain. And the noise of the cannon was of the noise of thunder in the heavens and the flashes of fires of their guns were like flashes of lightning."

Sejarah Melayu
(Malay Annals)

A Portuguese ship

The Sultan fighting on top of his elephant

Portuguese Voyages

In the 15th century, Portuguese rulers initiated voyagers of discovery on land and sea. One of the aims of these voyagers was to buy spices from Asia. The Venetians had sold them spices who, in turn, bought them from the Muslims in Egypt and Syria. Because of their long revolt against Muslim rule in their country, the Portuguese were anti-Muslim and fanatical Christians. They now sought a direct route to the Spice Islands by-passing the Muslim traders.

Alfonso de Albuquerque

Alfonso de Albuquerque

In the early 16th century, Portugal was the most advanced maritime nation in Europe. Alfonso de Albuquerque became the governor of Portugal's Asian empire. He wanted to dominate the Muslim world and the spice trade. He had seized Goa the year before capturing Melaka. Four years on, he would conquer Hormuz in the Persian gulf.

The Battle

For one month, Albuquerque laid seige to Melaka with sixteen ships. The Sultan released Portuguese prisoners, promised to pay for Sequeira's losses and agreed to allow the Portuguese to built a fortress in Melaka. This was not enough for Albuquerque.

The Portuguese attacked, burning the city. As night fell, Albuquerque withdrew his forces. The Portuguese then used a tall armoured junk to capture the bridge. With the city and the Sultans forces divided in two, Melaka soon fell.

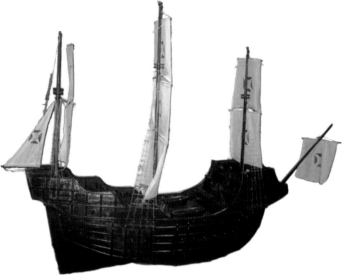

A model of the Flor de la Mer

Superior numbers

The Portuguese assault on Melaka involved 1,100 Portuguese men against Melaka's 20,000. However, the Portuguese were disciplined, well-trained and had better weapons. Their artillery outranged the Malay artillery. Albuquerque was an outstanding leader and military commander. The Melakan defenders had a low morale, many were untrained and many were foreigner mercenaries who did not want to fight. Their leaders were also divided.

An ornament from a Portuguese cannon

Eurasian Community

When the Portuguese conquered Melaka, Albuquerque encouraged his men to marry local women. Their descendants, the Eurasians (also know as 'Kristang'), lived in the Malay villages and adopted Malay customs. The Eurasians remained distinct from the Malays as they retained their Christian religion. Today, their language is a mix of Malay and Portuguese. Many Malay words have a Portuguese origin: bendera (flag), meja (table), almari (cupboard) and keju (cheese).

Key Dates

1498 - Vasco da Gama reaches India

1509 - Sequeira arrives in Melaka

1511 - Portugal captures Melaka

Flor de la Mer

With Melaka conquered, the Portuguese put the city's treasures on a ship called the *Flor de La Mer* ("Flower of the Sea"). Bound for Portugal, the treasures were to be presented to the Portuguese king.

These included:

- six bronze lions from the royal graves
- jewelry
- brocaded howdahs (a howdah is a seat with a canopy for riding on top of an elephant)
- gold-plated palanquins

The vessel also carried many Melakan embroiderers, young girls and youths from noble families, all to be sent to Portugal as slaves. Just off Sumatra, the ship sank and all its treasures and people were lost.

A'Formosa

A'Formosa (which means 'The Famous') was the fort which the Portuguese built in Melaka after they captured the city. Built at the foot of a hill near the mouth of Melaka river, it had 2.4 metre wide walls. Other than residences for the Portuguese officials it contained a town hall, five churches and two hospitals. The fort was demolished by the British and the Santiago Gate is all that remains today.

The Santiago Gate is the last remains of the Portuguese fort today. It was located at its eastern end.
(see arrow)

Map of the Portuguese Fort in Melaka

Find Out More

Melaka Empire
Dutch Influence
Aceh Attacks

Prehistory

Prehistory refers to a period in the past when there were no historical records. This means that we can only find information through digging up old sites and examining human remains. This was a time called the Stone Age, a time of primitive humans. Their weapons and tools were made from stone, bone and wood.

Stone Age humans lived in the Niah Caves, Sarawak. We know this because a 38,000 year-old skull was found there. They also lived in the caves of Perak where a 10,000 year old human skeleton was discovered. In Gua Cha, Kelantan, there is a rock shelter that was used to bury the dead 20,000 years ago. Stone Age sites have also been found in Kedah.

People may have arrived here from South China via Taiwan or Thailand. They would have spread to the many islands especially when the sea levels were low and many islands were part of the mainland.

"South-East Asia today is an anthropologist's paradise. In its mountains and jungles live the remnants of a great variety of peoples."

D.G.E. Hall
A History of South-East Asia

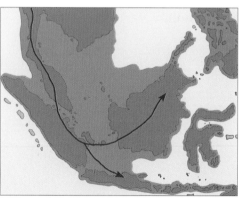

The shaded area shows the dry land about 18,000 years ago. This allowed humans to settle in the islands of today.

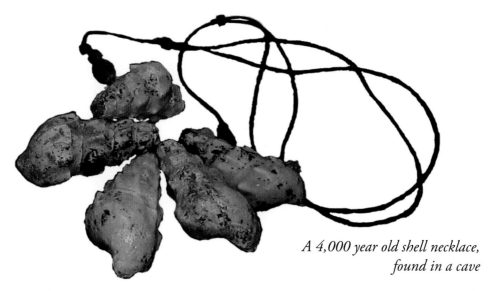

A 4,000 year old shell necklace, found in a cave

Early Arrivals

One of the first peoples to arrive on the Malay peninsula were the Austro-asiatics. These ancestors of the Semang arrived about 12,000 years ago. They lived in small family groups in limestone caves. They used primitive stone tools, hunted animals, fished and gathered food from plants. They also traded their forest products.

The next group of people to settle were the ancestors of the Senoi. They lived in villages, practised agriculture, had polished stone tools and even made pottery.

This 10,000 year old skeleton is called the "Perak Man". He was buried in a cave with food, shells and stone tools.

Austronesian arrivals

The Austronesians arrived on the Malay peninsula 4,500 years ago. Austronesians were better at agriculture that the earlier arrivals. They lived in large villages and had domesticated animals. Some were headhunters and cannibals. They also put up megaliths, used jars and dolmens to bury their dead. They were skillful in sea navigation. They are the ancestors of the Malays and many other island peoples. Borneo's indigenous peoples are all Austronesian. This is different from the Malay peninsula where its indigenous peoples are a mix of Austro-asiatics and Austronesians.

Austronesian Languages

The Austronesians may have spread to many places, including what is now the Philippines, Malaysia, Indonesia and the islands of the Pacific Ocean. This is because the languages in those places belong to the same language family as the Austronesians.

Find Out More

Rebellion Against British Rule

In the 19th century, Britain ruled over much of the Malay peninsula. The locals did not have the military might to oust the British from their lands but they did rebel against British rule.

After Francis Light settled in Penang, Sultan Abdullah of Kedah tried to retake the island because Britain broke its promises. Two hundred years later, when British Residents had control of three Malay states, the local chiefs killed James Birch, the British Resident in Perak. In Negri Sembilan, Yamtuan Antah, Datuk Bandar and Abdul Said had, at various times, all fought against British soldiers. The chiefs in Pahang also rebelled in the Pahang War. In North Borneo, Mat Salleh fought against British power. In Sarawak, the Ibans rebelled against the White Rajahs.

Although all these counter-attacks and uprisings were unsuccessful, it showed that the locals were willing to fight against British rule.

"The British used every means to assert their power in the Malay States. When dissident chiefs opposed [their rule], fire-power was used to subdue them . . ."

Khoo Kay Kim
Malay Society

Raja Abdullah (left) was exiled to the Seychelles. Yamtuan Antah (right) was exiled to Singapore

The British had well-trained solidiers and better weapons

Naning War

Naning was one of the states of Negri Sembilan. When the Dutch ruled Melaka, Naning paid an annual tribute to the Dutch. When the English took over Melaka, they demanded the same tribute. Abdul Said, the chief of Naning, refused. The British then sent 150 soldiers to arrest him but Naning resisted. There were no roads and the British had to fight in swamps and paddy fields. They were constantly ambushed and so were forced to retreat.

The British leaders were too ashamed to be defeated by the tiny state of Naning and so sent a larger force. This time Abdul Said was defeated and was sent to Melaka where he lived until his death. It cost the British a huge amount of money to capture Naning only to collect a very small payment.

Perak War

After the Pangkor Treaty, James Birch became the first British Resident of Perak. The Raja of Perak and his chiefs soon argued with Birch. The locals thought that Birch would have limited powers but Birch felt he could do as he liked. Birch wanted to end debt-slavery and the chiefs' rights to collect taxes.

With support from the Ruler and Chiefs, Maharaja Lela killed Birch at Pasir Salak. The British sent 300 troops from Singapore, India and Hong Kong to catch the culprits. Maharaja Lela was executed. Raja Abdullah, the ruler, and Ngah Ibrahim, the chief of Larut, were sent into exile in the Seychelles. Raja ismail, who had claimed to be Perak's ruler, was exiled in Johor. The British then made Raja Yusuf Perak's new ruler.

Tok Janggut Rebellion
1915

Sultan Abdullah
1791

Perak War
1875

Pahang War
1891-1895

Rebellion
Locations

Naning War
1831-1832

Datuk Bandar &
Yamtuan Antah
1874 - 1875

Pahang War

Under British pressure, in 1888 Sultan Ahmad (formerly Wan Ahmad) took a British Resident. The local chiefs protested at not being able to collect taxes and took up arms against the British. They were led by Dato' Bahaman, but it was a fighter called Mat Kilau who became a legend because of his bravery. The Orang Asli or indigenous people also helped fight against British soldiers. The uprising, however, was eventually put down.

Key Dates

1831 - Naning War

1849 - Iban Uprising against Rajah Brooke

1874 - James Birch killed

1874 - Datuk Bandar defeated by British troops

1891 - 1895 The Pahang War

1895 - 1905 - Mat Salleh Rebellion

1915 - Tok Janggut Rebellion

Find Out More

Dutch Influence
British Control
Borneo

Datuk Bandar

Sungai Ujong, a state in Negri Sembilan, fell into turmoil. Two chiefs, Datuk Kelana and Datuk Bandar argued over who could tax the boats on the Linggi river. Datuk Bandar's men blocked the river which stopped the flow of tin to Melaka. Traders in Melaka lost money and complained to the British.

The British wanted to re-open the river and gave Datuk Kelana weapons to fight Datuk Bandar. Instead Datuk Bandar defeated Datuk Kelana. To get more British help, Datuk Kelana agreed to take a British Resident. The British then sent in their soldiers and Datuk Bandar was defeated. The British made Datuk Kelana the chief of Sungei Ujong and exiled Datuk Bandar to Singapore.

Tok Janggut

The Sultan of Kelantan had accepted a British advisor. This meant that the British were now responsible for levying taxes and the traditional chiefs could no longer do so. Tok Janggut, whose real name was Haji Mat Hassan, persuaded the villagers not to pay tax to the British. When a police officer was sent to arrest Tok Janggut, Tok Janggut stabbed him to death and burnt buildings and houses of several European planters. Two hundred soldiers were sent from Singapore. Tok Janggut fought them but was shot and killed.

Yamtuan Antah

Tunku Antah had made himself ruler of Negri Sembilan but the important chiefs disagreed. In 1875, he attacked the British forces at Bukit Putus but he too was defeated. The British also sent him into exile in Singapore but, later, they allowed him to return. He then only ruled in Seri Menanti, the royal village and its surroundings, until his death.

REBELLION IN BORNEO

Mat Salleh Rebellion

There had been several uprisings against the British Chartered Company in North Borneo. The most serious one was when Mat Salleh, a man of mixed Bajau and Sulu parentage, led a five-year-war against the British. The locals held him in awe and thought he could produce flames from his mouth and lighting from his cleaver. He was killed in 1900 but jungle warfare carried on for another five years.

Iban Uprising

A Malay called Laksamana led the Ibans of the Saribas River against the Brooke rule in Sarawak. More than a thousand Ibans were killed, ninety-eight of their boats destroyed and many villages burnt. The White Rajah had help from the British navy and the Ibans were defeated. He built forts on these rivers to stop the Ibans attacking boats.

Riau-Johor

After the Portuguese invaded Melaka, the Melakan royal family and chiefs fled to the island of Bintan (also known as 'Riau'). Thus began the new kingdom of Riau-Johor.

Riau-Johor had a difficult start as it fought against Acehnese and Portuguese attacks in the 16th century. Eventually, it became powerful enough to help the Dutch capture Melaka from the Portuguese. Later, Riau-Johor thrived as a trading centre.

When its sultan was murdered, the Bendahara declared himself sultan. Then Raja Kechil captured the kingdom and became ruler. Next, the Bugis from Selangor ousted Raja Kechil and became the real power behind the throne.

To control trade in the region, the Bugis fought two wars against the Dutch but eventually the Dutch took over Riau-Johor. Eventually, they deposed the Sultan and the kingdom was lost.

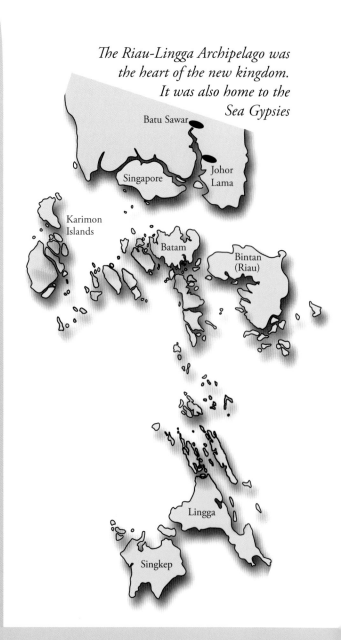

The Riau-Lingga Archipelago was the heart of the new kingdom. It was also home to the Sea Gypsies

Batu Sawar

Singapore

Johor Lama

Karimon Islands

Batam

Bintan (Riau)

Lingga

Singkep

Body armour was used by both Malays and Bugis in the conflict

The Melaka Bloodline

The Melaka Sultans were seen as divine rulers. Sultan Mahmud was its eighth and last ruler. After the Portuguese invaded Melaka, he became Riau-Johor's first sultan. His descendants ruled the kingdom until 1699, when Megat Sri Rama murdered its cruel sultan, Sultan Mahmud III. The Melaka bloodline did not end with the Sultan's death though. After the Portuguese invaded Melaka, Sultan Mahmud's brother became the ruler in Perak. He took the name Sultan Muzaffar Shah. Sultan Muzaffar Shah's descendants still rule Perak today.

The New Ruler

Sultan Abdul Jalil, the former Bendahara, became ruler after Sultan Mahmud II was murdered. However, Sultan Abdul Jalil was not regarded by the people as a divine ruler. This was because he did not share the bloodline as the Melakan rulers who had ruled for the past three hundred years.

Raja Kechil's Brief Reign

Raja Kechil from Sumatra claimed to be the son of the murdered Sultan and, therefore, a divine prince. With support from the Sea Gypsies, he attacked and captured Riau-Johor. He demoted the new ruler, Sultan Abdul Jalil, back to Bendahara. The Bendahara fled to Pahang but was murdered by Raja Kechil's men. Raja Kechil ruled for three years until the Bugis ousted him. He tried several times to recapture Riau-Johor but failed.

A Sea Gypsy house boat

Enter the Bugis

The Bugis led by Daeng Parani from Selangor captured Bintan in 1721. His warriors were chain-clad and used muskets and blunderbusses. Raja Kechil, who had taken over as ruler from Sultan Abdul Jalil, fled and started a new kingdom in Siak, Sumatra.

The Bugis made sure that the position of Yamtuan Muda or Under King would always be held by a Bugis. They would be the real rulers. The sultans, descendants of Sultan Abdul Jalil, became sultans with no power. The first sultan under the Bugis was Sultan Abdul Jalil's 20 year old son, Sulaiman.

Throughout his life Sultan Sulaiman was to struggle unsuccessfully against the Bugis for power in his kingdom.

The End of Riau-Johor

After the second Bugis-Dutch war, the Dutch took control of Riau-Johor. In 1787, wanting to expel the Dutch, Sultan Mahmud III asked Ilanun pirates from Sulu to capture Bintan. Worried about a Dutch attack, he then fled to the island of Lingga. From then on his descendants would be known as Sultans of Lingga. The Dutch returned to Bintan and took control of Riau-Johor. The Anglo-Dutch treaty of 1824 split the kingdom between the Dutch and the British which further weakened it. In 1911, the Dutch deposed the last sultan and the kingdom of Riau-Johor came to an end.

Three Sultan Mahmuds

Sultan Mahmud I
ruled 1488-1528 → Last Sultan of Melaka and first Sultan of Riau-Johor

Sultan Mahmud II
ruled 1685-1699 → Last of the Melaka bloodline. He was cruel and was killed.

Sultan Mahmud III
ruled 1761-1812 → Fled to Lingga and was its first Sultan.

Key Dates

1699 - Sultan Mahmud II is murdered, his Bendahara becomes ruler

1718 - Raja Kechil captures Riau-Johor and becomes its ruler

1721 - Bugis capture Riau-Johor and install their own Under King (Yamtuan Muda)

1785 - Riau-Johor ruled by the Dutch

1911 - Last Sultan of Lingga deposed by the Dutch

The Dutch gave this cannon to the Sultan of Riau-Johor. It was then given to the Acehnese but later seized by the British.

Conquest & Marriage

As the Malay kingdoms were fought over, conquest and marriage went hand in hand. When Raja Kechil captured Riau-Johor he married Sultan Abdul Jalil's younger daughter. In turn, when the Bugis ousted Raja Kechil and took control of the kingdom, one Bugis leader married Sultan Abdul Jalil's eldest daughter whilst another married the sultan's sister. This ensured that the descendants of these foes would be related. The new Bugis Yamtuan Muda, Daeng Merewah, harked back further and married the wife of the murdered Sultan Mahmud II.

New Kingdoms

The Sultan of Riau-Johor was under Dutch control whilst his territories, Johor and Pahang, were controlled by the British. After a civil war in Pahang (1858-1863), Wan Ahmad became its Bendahara. In 1885, both the Temenggung of Johor, Maharaja Abu Bakar, and the Bendahara of Pahang took the title of Sultan. Both territories became new kingdoms.

Sultan Abu Bakar, first Sultan of Johor. He was formerly its Temenggong. He had also used the title of 'Maharaja'.

The Bendahara's Dynasty

Bendahara Abdul Majid's descendants today rule the sultanates of Johor, Terengganu and Pahang. In 1824 Riau-Johor was split between the British and Dutch. This allowed the Temenggong in Johor and the Bendahara in Pahang to become sultans. Both were descendants of Abdul Jalil.

Bendahara Abdul Majid
died 1697

Sultan Abdul Jalil
Sultan of Riau-Johor
1699-1719

Sultan Zainal Abidin
Sultan of Trengganu
1725-1733

Sultans of Trengganu

Tun Abbas
Bendahara of Riau-Johor

Temenggung Abdul Jamal

Bendahara Abdul Majid

Sultan Abu Bakar
Sultan of Johor
1885-1895

Sultan Ahmad Shah
Sultan of Pahang
1887-1914

Sultans of Johor

Sultans of Pahang

Find Out More

Bugis
Dutch Influence
Pahang Civil War

Second World War

At the end of 1941, just before the bombing of Pearl Harbour, Japanese troops landed in southern Thailand and northern Malaya and captured several airfields.

Allied troops were sent to fight the Japanese but withdrew as the invaders attacked. The Allied troops were ill-equipped, poorly trained and unprepared.

With Japanese soldiers rapidly advancing, the Allies abandoned Penang. As the Allies retreated further, the Japanese soon captured Kuala Lumpur. Allied troops then defended the south at Gemas and ambushed the Japanese. Still the Japanese pressed on and the Allies withdrew to Singapore.

Singapore fell on 15 February 1942. The Japanese with shocking speed had seized Malaya from the British. Their troops were better trained and battle-hardened and their ships and planes ruled sea and sky.

"There was no way that Malaya could fight off a full-scale atttack from the air, on the land, or from the sea. Apart from a sickening lack of defences or equipment, the troops were not in a state of readiness."

Lynette Ramsay Silver
The Bridge at Parit Sulong

British anti-aircraft gun

British Commanding Officer, General Percival, on his way to surrender to the Japanese commander, General Yamashita. General Yamashita became known as the "Tiger of Malaya"

The Japanese Zero fighter plane was much faster and heavily-armed than the Allies' Buffalo fighters

Repulse **and** *Prince of Wales*

Two days after the Japanese invasion of Malaya, the British warships – the *Repulse* and the *Prince of Wales* – were sent from Singapore to attack the Japanese. The aircraft carrier, the *Indomitable*, which was supposed to accompany them had run aground. Without aircraft protection, the two warships were easily sunk by Japanese planes. This was a severe blow to British and Malayan morale.

Japan's Motives

Japan wanted to create an East Asia which they ruled over. Their slogan was "Asia for the Asians". This meant removing Western domination. Japan's main motive though was to exploit Malaya's economy for its military expansion. They were unsuccesful as the retreating British destroyed roads, bridges, railways and vital equipment in the rubber and tin industry.

Key Dates

1941 - 8 December, Japanese troops land in Kota Bharu

1942 - 7 January, Japanese capture Kuala Lumpur

1942 - 15 February, Singapore falls to the Japanese

1945 - 12 September, formal Japanese surrender in Singapore

Japanese Invasion

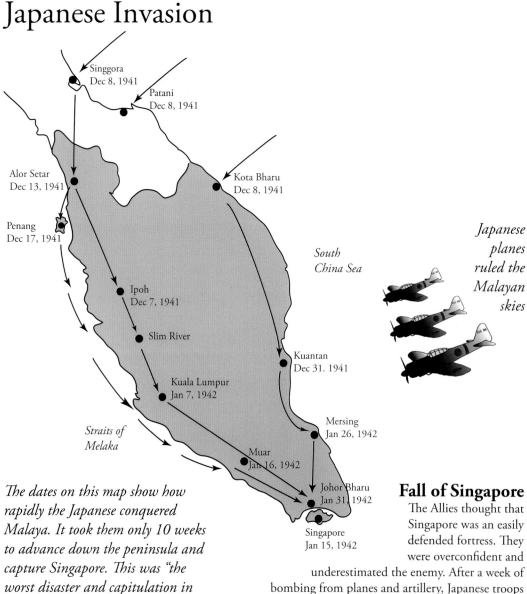

Singgora
Dec 8, 1941

Patani
Dec 8, 1941

Alor Setar
Dec 13, 1941

Kota Bharu
Dec 8, 1941

Penang
Dec 17, 1941

*South
China Sea*

*Japanese
planes
ruled the
Malayan
skies*

Ipoh
Dec 7, 1941

Slim River

Kuantan
Dec 31. 1941

Kuala Lumpur
Jan 7, 1942

Mersing
Jan 26, 1942

*Straits of
Melaka*

Muar
Jan 16, 1942

Johor Bharu
Jan 31, 1942

Singapore
Jan 15, 1942

The dates on this map show how rapidly the Japanese conquered Malaya. It took them only 10 weeks to advance down the peninsula and capture Singapore. This was "the worst disaster and capitulation in British history" wrote British Prime Minister Winston Churchill.

Fall of Singapore

The Allies thought that Singapore was an easily defended fortress. They were overconfident and underestimated the enemy. After a week of bombing from planes and artillery, Japanese troops landed in Singapore and soon swept away the Allies' defences. The Japanese reached the centre of the island and captured ammunition and petrol dumps. The Allies now only controlled the city and port. Low on food, water and ammunition, the exhausted Allies surrendered.

Find Out More

British Control
Emergency
Independence

The Occupation

The Japanese occupied British Malaya, British North Borneo and Sarawak. Under their cruel occupation, the locals soon hated the Japanese. Prices skyrocketed due to shortages and the massive printing of money. One example is that whilst an egg cost 3 cents in 1941, it shot up to $35 in 1945. Food was scarce and the economy stalled. The Chinese suffered the worst because the Japanese were at war with China, and so regarded the Chinese as enemies. More than 100,000 locals may have died under Japanese rule.

Armed Resistance

During the Japanese occupation, a group of armed guerillas fought the Japanese, They were mainly Chinese and called themselves the Malayan Peoples Anti Japanese Army (MPAJA) They were given supplies and arms by the British. When the Japanese surrendered at the end of the Second World War, the British returned to Malaya.

Death Railway

When Malaya fell, the Japanese captured around 85,000 soldiers. Many were imprisoned in Changi in Singapore. As the shipping lanes were threatened by the Allies, the Japanese needed to built a railway from Thailand into Burma to supply their troops there. Of the 50,000 prisoners sent to construct the railway, only 30,000 survived. A third of the 270,000 Asian civilians died building it. Many of them were civilian Indian plantation workers. Disease, malnutrition and mistreatment were the main causes of death.

Allied trench mortar and sandbags

Casualties

It is estimated that 166,600 British Commonwealth troops were either killed or captured by the Japanese when they invaded Malaya. The Japanese loss less men, which is estimated at 15,000.

War memorial

Siamese Invasion of Kedah

Kedah was Siam's vassal state. In the early 19th century, under Siam's orders, Kedah invaded and captured Perak.

The Siamese then demanded from Kedah war-supplies for its war against Burma. Kedah though could not afford it and so Siam attacked it. Many Malays were cruelly killed and the kingdom devastated. Siam tried to invade Perak but, with Selangor's help, the Siamese retreated.

Because of the Anglo-Siamese Treaty, the British in Penang could not help Kedah. Kedah was left on its own and for twenty years its people tried to retake their kingdom.

In 1831, Kedah's forces captured Kedah for six months but was driven out. Several years later their forces again recaptured their kingdom and even invaded Siamese territory. Siam counter attacked and recaptured Kedah.

After twenty years in exile, the Siamese king finally allowed the Sultan of Kedah to return to his kingdom.

"The Siamese army under the command of the Raja of Ligor ... invaded Kedah. In a short campaign the country was laid waste with great loss of life and many atrocities."

J. Kennedy
A History of Malaya

The 'Bunga Mas dan Perak' were beautifully decorative flowers shaped by expert Malay craftsmen using gold and silver. It was a tribute given annually by the northern Malay kingdoms to Siam. It acknowledged that Siam was the suzerain or overlord and the northern Malay kingdoms were its vassals.

Find Out More

Penang
British Control
Pahang Civil War

Kedah fighters waged guerilla warfare against the Siamese

Anglo Siamese Treaty

After the Siamese invaded Kedah, they wanted to attack Perak and Selangor. The British knew that this would disrupt trade and so signed this treaty (also known as the "Burney Treaty") with Siam. Under it the Siamese promised not to attack Perak and Selangor. The British also recognised that Kedah belonged to Siam. The British also had to promise that they would stop the Sultan from trying to recapture his kingdom.

Sultan in Exile

Sultan Ahmad Tajuddin, the Sultan of Kedah, attempted to recapture Kedah from the Siamese but failed. The British tried to stop his efforts by sending him to Melaka. In the end, the Siamese gave up trying to rule Kedah. After twenty years in exile, the Sultan returned to his kingdom. He passed away three years later.

New kingdom of Perlis

After capturing Kedah, Siam divided it into four parts: Kubang Pasu, Setul, Perlis and Kedah proper, each with its own chief. After the Sultan returned to his kingdom, Kubang Pasu became part of Kedah again but Perlis was still controlled by its chief – Sayid Husain Jamalullail. He later became a ruler with the title of 'Raja'. His descendants still rule Malaysia's smallest kingdom today. Setul was never returned and is still part of Thailand.

Elephants were used in the conflict

Key Dates

1816 - Under Siam's orders, Kedah invades Perak

1819 - Siam attacks Kedah

1826 - Anglo Siamese Treaty

1842 - Sultan Ahmad Tajuddin returns to Kedah as ruler

1845 - Sayid Husain Jamalullail becomes ruler of Perlis

Singapore

Thomas Stamford Raffles, an officer of the British East India Company, landed on Singapore to start a British settlement close to the Spice Islands.

When he arrived, there were a thousand Malays, Chinese and Sea Gypsies living there. He paid the local chief and the Sultan a yearly sum of money and began his settlement. Major William Farquhar became Singapore's first Resident.

The Dutch protested against the settlement. Singapore became a successful free port with many new migrants, mostly Chinese. With Singapore now a successful trading centre, the British refused to return it to the Dutch.

The British and Dutch then signed the Anglo-Dutch Treaty which recognised Singapore as belonging to Britain.

Singapore became part of the Straits Settlements. It joined the Federation of Malaysia but was later expelled.

"... the seas around Singapore were feared ... Whenever [the pirates] plundered a ship ... they shared the spoils and slaughtered the crew. All along the shore there were hundreds of human skulls rolling about on the sand [Colonel Farquhar] ordered them them to be gathered up and cast into the sea."

Munshi Abdullah

A painting of Raffles at 36. He founded the British settlement a year later.

Find Out More

Riau-Johor
Second World War
Malaysia and Confrontation

Singapore's Name

Temasik means 'sea town' in the old Malay language. Legend has it that Paramesvara, the ruler of Temasik, one day strolled into the jungle and saw a three-coloured lion from Hindu mythology, called a 'Singa'. 'Pura' meant 'city' in the old Malay language and so Paramesvara changed the name of Temasik to 'Singapura', which is anglacised as 'Singapore'.

Why a Sultan of Singapore?

Singapore was part of the kingdom of Riau-Johor and ruled by its Temenggong. He gave Raffles permission to start a British settlement there but the Yamtuan Muda, who controlled the Sultan, refused. Raffles got around the problem by declaring that the Sultan's elder brother was the Sultan of Singapore. This new ruler, Sultan Hussein, in turn, gave Raffles permission to start a British settlement there.

Separation

Almost a century and a half after Raffles landed in Singapore, its people agreed to join the Federation of Malaysia. After Malaysia was formed, there were problems between Singapore's PAP party and Malaya's Alliance coalition. Racial violence broke out in Singapore. Because of a threat of more racial violence, Singapore was expelled from Malaysia and so it became an independent nation.

Singapore's Lee Kwan Yew in Malaysia's new Parliament House

Key Dates

1819 - British settlement in Singapore

1824 - Anglo-Dutch Treaty

1959 - Self rule in Singapore

1963 - Singapore joins Malaysia

1965 - Singapore is expelled

Srivijaya Empire

The Srivijaya empire was a Mahayana Buddhist civilisation which existed for 700 years. Its kings bore the title 'Sri Maharaja'.

Srivijaya's capital was in Palembang, Sumatra. Ships from Arabia, Persia and India sailed into South East Asia to buy spices and rain forest produce; and to sell their own wares. As they had to sail through the seas controlled by Srivijaya, the kingdom would tax these ships. Srivijaya also kept its waters safe from pirates. Soon vessels went there to trade and so the kingdom became an emporium.

Srivijaya, now a wealthy maritime empire, ruled over all the coastal ports, towns and villages on the Malay peninsula and Sumatra. Although an overlord of all the surrounding kingdoms, the empire too had an overlord – China.

Cultured, civilised and a centre of religion, the Srivijaya empire was greatly respected by other kingdoms.

"[Srivijaya] left only an insignificant number of [monuments] because its kings were busier watching over trade in the Straits than building temples or having their praises carved in stone."

George Coèdes
Sriwijaya: History, Religion and Language of an early Malay polity

This inscribed stone, with seven cobra heads on top, was found near Palembang. Water was poured over the stone and collected at the bottom spout. Srivijaya's vassal kings would drink the water and swear allegiance to Srivijaya.

Mahayana Buddhism

Srivijaya was a religious centre of Mahayana Buddhism, a religion that combined Buddhist and Hindu teachings. Srivijayans were Mahayana Buddhist. To support the religion, its kings even built temples in India. The earliest Mahayana Buddhist inscription was found in Kedah from the 6th century and another in Palembang dated 684.

Srivijaya was a centre of Mahayana Buddhism

A Malay empire

The court ceremonies, laws and religion of Srivijaya had come from India. Yet Srivijaya is known as a Malay empire because many Malays in Malaysia are descended from Srivijayans. The traditions, customary laws and language of the Malays can also be traced back to the Srivijaya Empire. This culture continued on the Malay peninsula through the Melaka empire which passed the same traditions to the other Malay sultanates on the peninsula.

The river Melayu

Melayu river flows through Djambi, once a capital of Srivijaya. The people living there called themselves Melayu. Melayu is anglacised into the word "Malay". So the Malays of Malaysia take their name from a Sumatran river.

Malay ideas of kingship originate from Srivijaya

Visit by I-Tsing

In 671, the Chinese pilgrim, I-Tsing visited Srivijaya where he found a thousand Buddhist monks. He stayed for six months before heading to India to further study the religion. He returned to Srivijaya to translate Buddhist texts from Sanskrit into Chinese.

張文明

Key Dates

7th-13th century: Srivijaya Empire

1025 - Chola attacks Srivijaya

1275 - Majapahit captures Srivijaya

An example of a Srivijayan inscription. Only five inscriptions have been found so far. They use an Indian alphabet and Sanskrit words.

Javanese Links

Around the mid-ninth century, perhaps through marriage or family links, Srivijaya was ruled by a Sailendra king, Balaputradeva. The Sailendras were Javanese kings who had built many architectural monuments in Java, including the famous Borobodur.

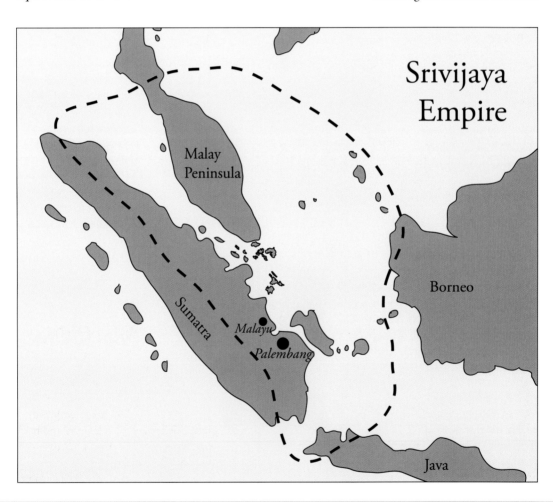

Remains of a 12th century Hindu temple found in Bujang valley, Kedah. Kedah was once a vassal state of Srivijaya.

"Princes of Srivijaya presented gifts of dwarfs, musicians and multi-coloured parrots to the Emperor of China. The Emperor then bestowed titles of honour on the King of Srivijaya."

Decline of Srivijaya

From the 11th century onwards, Srivijaya had lost much of its power. It began when Chola, an empire from Southern India, attacked it and captured its king, Sangrama Vijayottungavarman. Srivijaya was left weak. Combined with a lot less trade from China, the empire was not as wealthy as before.

Two Kingdoms

Chinese records from the 7th century mention two kingdoms. One was "Mo-lo-yeou" which is Malayu, now known as Jambi. The other was "Che-li-fo-che" which is Srivijaya, located at Palembang. Old Malay inscriptions state that Srivijaya had conquered Malayu and was preparing to attack Java. From then on Srivijaya's power grew into a wealthy empire.

End of Srivijaya

Srivijaya faced threats from both Siam to its north and Majapahit to its east. In 1275 the Majapahit king in Java launched his fleets against Srivijaya. After a lengthy and hard war, Srivijaya was defeated. By the 14th century, Srivijaya had become a vassal state of Majapahit.

Find Out More

Early Kingdoms
Melaka Empire
Paramesvara

99

Tin Mine Wars

For centuries the Malays have mined tin on a small scale. In the mid 19th century large tin deposits were found in Perak and Selangor and, at the same time, there was a huge demand for the ore overseas.

The local Malays knew this would bring great wealth but they did not have the means to mine the huge deposits. So they asked the businessmen in the Straits Settlements for help. These businessmen brought in thousands of labourers from Southern China to work the tin mines. These labourers soon organised themselves into secret societies, the two main ones being the Ghee Hins and, their enemies, the Hai Sans.

The Malay chiefs became rich and powerful which caused problems for the rulers of these states. It eventually led to civil war with the secret societies taking opposing sides.

In the end, peace returned only after the British took control of Perak and Selangor.

Key Dates

1848 - Long Ja'afar invites the Chinese to mine his tin in Larut

1858 - His son, Ngah Ibrahim becomes chief of Larut

1862 - Ghee Hin and Hai San gang war in Larut

1872 - Ghee Hin and Hai San resume fighting

1874 - Pangkor Treaty

Perak Tin Mine War

Larut, which today is known as Taiping, was rich in tin. Its chief, Ngah Ibrahim, was wealthy and powerful. After the ruler of Perak died, Ngah Ibrahim helped Raja Ismail become the new ruler. Raja Abdullah, the heir apparent, felt cheated and, with Ghee Hin's help, he captured Ngah Ibrahim's Larut mines. Then Ngah Ibrahim, with Hai San support, re-captured his mines. Next, Raja Abdullah's forces blockaded the coast and stopped all tin from leaving Larut. The businessmen from the Straits Settlements, Chinese and British, lost money and so the British government stepped in. With the Pangkor Treaty, Perak fell into British hands and peace returned.

Selangor Tin Mine War

Raja Mahdi's father was the chief of Kelang. When he died, the Sultan of Selangor made someone else chief. Because Raja Mahdi's family lost control of its tin mines, Raja Mahdi attacked Kelang and took them over. Tunku Kudin, acting for the Sultan and with help from the Hai San, recaptured Kelang. In revenge, Raja Mahdi and the Ghee Hins seized the Hai San tin mines in Ampang. Then Kudin and the Hai San, led by Yap Ah Loy, attacked Raja Mahdi and re-took the Ampang mines. Ultimately, Kudin won as he had British support but it also led to Britain taking control of Selangor.

Yap Ah Loy

Secret Societies

Secret societies in China were political organisations. On the Malay Peninsula, however, they were set up for economic and social reasons. The Chinese called them *Kongsi*, or co-operatives. The secret society had a positive side: it helped members, gave them security and a sense of belonging. Its negative side was that it demanded total loyalty. Some carried out their own trials and handed down punishment on members, including the death penalty.

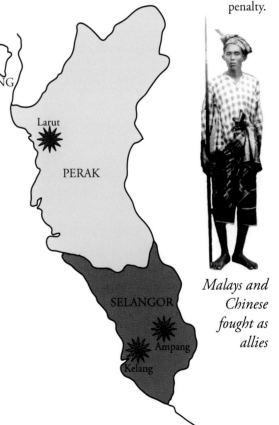

Malays and Chinese fought as allies

Find Out More

Pahang Civil War
British Control
Chinese

*This minature brass cannon resembles
a crocodile. It is from the kingdom of
Brunei, which then included Sabah
and Sarawak. Before money became
common, these cannons were used in
exchange for goods.*

Time Chart to History

How the Time Chart Works ...

This time chart gives you a bird's eye view of Malaysia's history. From the 1st to the 21 centuries, you'll find that all major events are found here.

However, not everything is recorded as there would be too many to include. But you will discover the main historic events for each entity.

So what these entities?

These are usually kingdoms or political units which through time, form larger ones or break off into smaller units. It depends on where you are on the time chart.

If you examine the full historical time chart two pages on, you will see it begins with six entities. Each entity follows a different time path.

Follow that entity to examine the events that affect it. Such events may cause the entity to break up into smaller entities. However, it may also join up with others entities, forming a larger one.

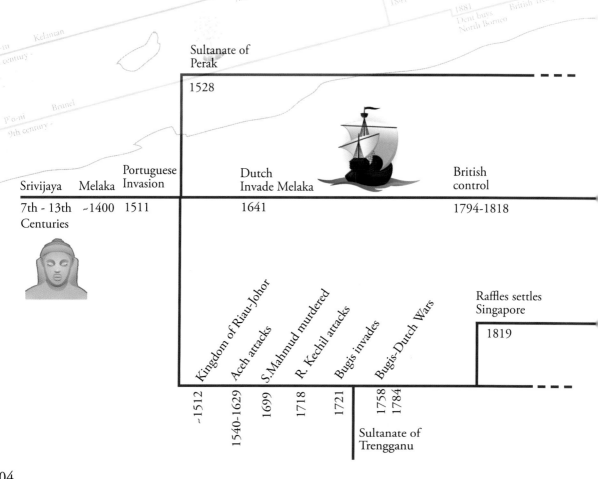

Example: following the red time line

This timeline, reproduced below, begins with **Srivijaya**. It leads us to Melaka as this is where Paramesvara flees too and begins his new kingdom. After the Portuguese invade Melaka, the line breaks off to form 2 other entities: Perak and Riau-Johor.

Let us follow **Melaka**'s time line for the moment. It shows that the Dutch invade Portuguese Melaka. Later the British take control of Melaka.

Now the red line has merged with other entities to form the dark blue line. Melaka has become part of the **Straits Settlements**. We continue to follow the dark blue line to see how Melaka becomes part of independent Malaya.

Let us retrace our steps to just after the Portuguese invasion.

If we follow the line upwards we discover that the Sultanate of **Perak** is formed. From here we can trace Perak's history.

Let us follow the timeline downwards instead. Here we see that the Kingdom of **Riau-Johor** is created. This kingdom battles Aceh, Raja Kechil and finally the Bugis invade. They in turn fight the Dutch who take control of the kingdom.

Notice how the red line now splits into three. The first split reveals that the new Sultanate of Trengganu is formed. The second split shows that Raffles takes control of Singapore from Riau-Johor. Singapore eventually joins Melaka and becomes part of the Straits Settlements.

By following the time chart we can discover much of Malaysia's history.

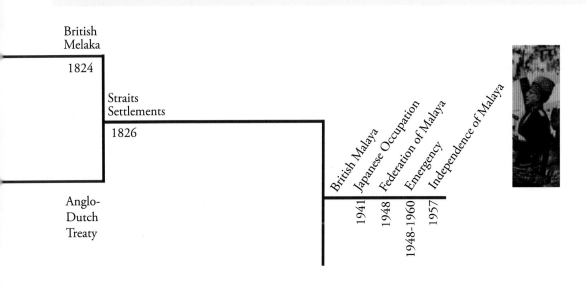

British Melaka

1824

Straits Settlements

1826

Anglo-Dutch Treaty

British Malaya — 1941
Japanese Occupation — 1948
Federation of Malaya — 1948-1960
Emergency — 1957
Independence of Malaya

Bugis migration
to Selangor

Sultanate of
Selangor

1680 onwards

1766

Minangkabau   Migration to
Kingdom   Rembau, S.Ujong etc.

Raja Ibrahim attacks
Dutch Melaka

Kingdom of
N. Sembilan

1347 - 1832   1400 onwards

1677

1721

Sultanate of
Perak

1528

Srivijaya   Melaka   Portuguese
                       Invasion

Dutch
Invade Melaka

British
control

7th - 13th   ~1400   1511
Centuries

1641

1794-1818

Light settles
Penang

1786

Raffles settles
Singapore

1819

Kingdom of Riau-Johor

Aceh attacks

S. Mahmud murdered

R. Kechil attacks

Bugis invades

Bugis-Dutch Wars

1512

1540-1629

1699

1718

1721

1758
1784

Sultanate of
Trengganu

Sultan Mansur
Shah dies

1725

1794

Langkasuka   Kadaram   Kedah

Civil War

Siamese
Invasion

1st century -   4th century -

1723-1724

1821

Chi-tu   Kelantan

Long Muhammad
is Sultan

6th century -

1800

P'o-ni   Brunei

9th century -

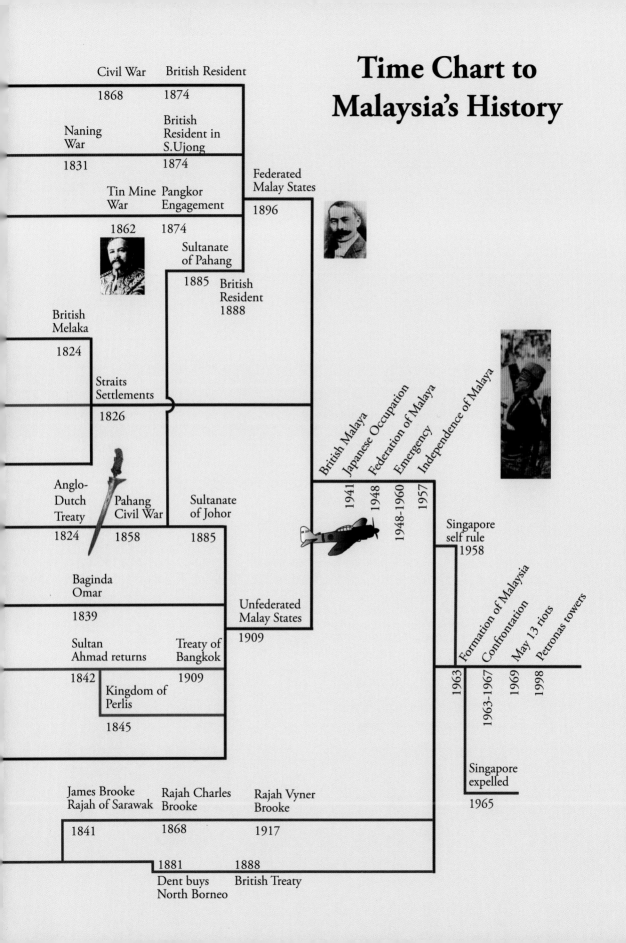

Time Chart to Malaysia's History

Civil War   British Resident
1868   1874

Naning   British
War   Resident in
                 S.Ujong
1831   1874

                          Federated
                          Malay States
Tin Mine Pangkor   1896
War   Engagement
1862   1874
                  Sultanate
                  of Pahang
                  1885   British
                          Resident
                          1888

British
Melaka
1824

Straits
Settlements
1826

Anglo-
Dutch   Pahang   Sultanate
Treaty   Civil War   of Johor
1824   1858   1885

Baginda
Omar
1839
                              Unfederated
Sultan   Treaty of   Malay States
Ahmad returns Bangkok   1909
1842   1909
              Kingdom of
              Perlis
              1845

British Malaya — 1941
Japanese Occupation — 1948
Federation of Malaya — 1948-1960
Emergency
Independence of Malaya — 1957

Singapore
self rule
1958

Formation of Malaysia — 1963
Confrontation — 1963-1967
May 13 riots — 1969
Petronas towers — 1998

Singapore
expelled
1965

James Brooke   Rajah Charles   Rajah Vyner
Rajah of Sarawak Brooke   Brooke
1841   1868   1917

1881   1888
Dent buys   British Treaty
North Borneo

This is a statue of the Hindu God Ganesha. It was found at Bujang Valley, the site of the old Hindu temples in south Kedah. Bujang Valley was an important trading centre in the 10th century.

Questions & Answers

Beginners Quiz

1. Which European power ruled over the Malay peninsula in the late 19th century?

   A. Portugal B. Holland
   C. Spain D. British

2. Which group of people migrated to the Malay peninsula from the Celebes?

   A. Bugis B. Minangkabau
   C. Javanese D. Acehnese

3. Why did the Dutch come to Asia?

   A. to sell spices B. to fight
   C. to preach D. to control the spice trade

4. What are megaliths?

   A. tall buildings B. large upright stones
   C. early kingdoms D. politicians

5. The Emergency began following?

   A. Independence B. Confrontation
   C. Second World War D. Separation

6. Which country granted Malaya it's independence?

   A. Holland B. Portugal
   C. America D. England

7. What is the Perak Man?

   A. a Pasir Salak warrior B. a stone memorial
   C. an old skeleton D. Perak's astronaut

8. Which country started the Confrontation against Malaysia?

   A. Brunei B. Singapore
   C. Philippines D. Indonesia

9. Which of these kingdoms was not an early kingdom on the Malay peninsula?

   A. Funan B. Kiu-li
   C. Chi-tu D. Langkasuka

10. Which of these people was a famous Kapitan China?

    A. Hang Li Po B. Yap Ah Loy
    C. Ghee Hin D. Tan Siew Sin

11. What was the former name of Sabah?

    A. Sarawak B. North Borneo
    C. Brunei D. Sulu

12. Who are the Orang Asli?

    A. migrants B. indigenous peoples
    C. a traditional music group D. tourists

13. The Pahang Civil War was a fight between?

    A. 2 strangers B. 2 sisters
    C. 2 brothers D. 2 cousins

14. Which royal family was Paramesvara a descendant of?

    A. Majapahit B. Pasai
    C. Minangkabau D. Srivijaya

15. Who leased Penang from the Kedah Sultan?

    A. Stamford Raffles B. Francis Light
    C. James Birch D. Frank Swettenham

16. Which was the first European power to invade Melaka?

    A. Spanish B. Dutch
    C. British D. Portuguese

17. Which kingdom conquered Pasai then attacked Portuguese Melaka and Riau-Johor?

    A. Holland B. Majapahit
    C. Aceh D. Minangkabau

18. Which commodity did Malaysia not usually export?

    A. Rubber B. Tin
    C. Whales D. Palm Oil

19. Who started a settlement in Singapore?

    A. Martin Lister B. Francis Light
    C. Stamford Raffles D. Hugh Clifford

20. How many states exist in Negri Sembilan?

    A. None B. Seven
    C. Nine D. Four

21. Why did ships stop at Melaka?

    A. to pray B. to trade
    C. to restock food D. to meet its ruler

22. What percentage of the population do in Malaysia do Indians make up?

    A. 10 percent B. 25 percent
    C. 2.5 percent D. 35 percent

23. Which commodity caused war in Selangor?

    A. gold B. silver
    C. tin D. rice

24. Which empire ruled over the Malay peninsula during the 7th to 13th centuries?

    A. Srivijaya B. Majapahit
    C. Siamese empire D. British empire

25. After the Portugese invasion, the Melaka Sultan began the new kingdom of?

    A. Kedah B. Riau-Johor
    C. Negri Sembilan D. Trengganu

26. Where did the Allies make a last stand against the Japanese?

    A. Singapore B. Penang
    C. Kuala Lumpur D. Melaka

ANSWERS
1.D 2.A 3.D 4.B 5.B 6.D 7.C 8.D
9.A 10.B 11.B 12.B 13.C 14.D
15.B 16.D 17.C 18.C 19.C 20.C
21.B 22.A 23.C 24.A 25.B 26.A

Intermediate Quiz

1. Which royal position did the Bugis appoint for themselves in Riau-Johor?

   A. Yamtuan Besar B. Yang DiPertua Negri
   C. Raja Kechil D. Yamtuan Muda

2. How long approximately did Paramesvara and his descendants rule Melaka?

   A. 150 years B. 100 years
   C. 250 years D. 200 years

3. Which was Melaka's most famous Bendahara?

   A. Tun Perak B. Bendahara Abdul Jalil
   C. Paramesvara D. Hang Tuah

4. How many White Rajahs were there?

   A. One B. Two
   C. Three D. Four

5. How long was the Kedah Sultan in exile before the Siamese allowed his return?

   A. 10 years B. 15 years
   C. 20 years D. 25 years

6. Which territory did not join Malaysia?

   A. Sabah B. Brunei
   C. Singapore D. Sarawak

7. Who was the first Sultan of Selangor?

   A. Yamtuan Antah B.Sultan Sulaiman
   C. Raja Lumu D. Sultan Abdullah

8. In which state was oil discovered off shore?

   A. Selangor B. Perlis
   C. Terengganu D. Penang

9. Which of these states was not part of the Straits Settlements?

   A. Singapore B. Selangor
   C. Melaka D. Penang

10. Who controlled Perak after the Perak Tin Mine War?

    A. the Hai Sans B. the Siamese
    C. the British D. the Malay chiefs

11. Which group is not a Malaysian Orang Asli tribe?

    A. Semang B. Senoi
    C. Proto-Malay D. Batak

12. Which religion did Langkasuka follow?

    A. Buddhism/Hinduism B. Islam
    C. Christianity D. Taoism

13. Who was the commander of the Portuguese forces invading Melaka?

    A. Diogo Lopes de Sequeira B. Barbosa
    C. Alfonso de Albuquerque D. H.N. Ridley

14. Malaysia expelled Singapore because of?

    A. over population B. poverty
    C. risk of racial violence D. war

15. The Indians call the Malay peninsula?

    A. land of silver B. land of gold
    C. land of diamonds D. land of tin

16. Who did the Communists assasinate?

    A. Henry Gurney B. James Birch
    C. Gerald Templar D. Frank Swettenham

17. Which conflict was <u>not</u> a rebellion against British rule?

    A. Pahang Civil War B. Naning War
    C. Iban Uprising D. Mat Salleh rebellion

18. Where are Malaysia's most famous "living stones" found?

    A. Pasir Salak B. Perlis
    C. Pangkor D. Pengkalan Kempas

19. Who was the founder of UMNO?

    A. Tun Razak B. Tun Mahathir
    C. Ja'afar Onn D. Tunku Abdul Rahman

20. Wan Ahmad & Wan Mutahir wanted to be?

    A. Laksamana B. Temenggong
    C. Bendahara D. Shah Bandar

21. Which state was <u>not</u> part of the Federated Malay States?

    A. Melaka B. Selangor
    C. Pahang D. Perak

22. Where was the kingdom of Pasai located?

    A. Next to Palembang B. Opposite Melaka
    C. Beside Singapore D. Beside Aceh

23. Which was Holland's main trading centre?

    A. Bencoolen B. Bintan
    C. Batavia D. Brunei

24. Which was Srivijaya's capital?

    A. Melaka B. Palembang
    C. Johor D. Aceh

25. What was the name of the British territory opposite Penang?

    A. Province Wellesley B. Rafflesia
    C. Prince of Wales D. Port Swettenham

26. In Stone Age times people could travel to the islands of today because?

    A. they mastered sailing B. sea levels were low
    C. they swam well D. they went as slaves

ANSWERS
1.D 2.B 3.A 4.C 5.C 6.B 7.C 8.C
9.B 10.C 11.D 12.A 13.C 14.C 15.B
16.A 17.A 18.D 19.C 20.C 21.A
22.D 23.C 24.B 25.A 26.B

Advanced Quiz

1. What does "Chi-tu" mean?

    A. yellow river place B. blue mountain ridge
    C. hazy muddy delta D. red earth land

2. Britain took over Sabah and Sarawak after the Second World War to?

    A. create Malaysia B. depose its Sultans
    C. help rebuild D. stop the Japanese

3. The Southern Chinese migrated to the Straits Settlements because of?

    A. political reasons B. war
    C. poverty D. secret society pressure

4. Which royal dynasty from the Malay peninsula were once rulers of Aceh?

    A. Negri Sembilan B. Terengganu
    C. Kedah D. Perak

5. Who signed the Pangkor Treaty for the British?

    A. Andrew Clarke B. James Low
    C. Hugh Clifford D. James Birch

6. Who was the first Bugis Under King for Riau-Johor?

    A. Daeng Parani B. Daeng Merewah
    C. Daeng Relaga D. Daeng Kemboja

7. What does the VOC stand for?

    A. Very Old Co. B. Dutch East India Co.
    C. East India Co. D. Vereenigne Open Co.

8. When did manufacturing grow strongly in Malaysia?

    A. Before 1950 B. 1950-1970
    C. 1970-1990 D. After 2000

9. What does the word "Semang" mean?

    A. servant B. soldier
    C. slave D. sailor

10. Which political party was not part of the Alliance coalition?

    A. Malayan Indian Congress B. UMNO
    C. Parti Negara D. MCA

11. The Trengganu stone contains Islamic inscriptions and is dated about?

    A. 1300 B. 1500
    C. 1641 D. Iron Age period

12. Which armed conflict was a fight against Chartered Company rule?

    A. Mat Salleh rebellion B. Iban Uprising
    C. Tok Janggut rebellion D. Naning War

13. The Portuguese at A'Formosa had 2 hospitals, five churches and ...?

    A. a memorial lake B. a cathedral
    C. a town hall D. a parliament

14. The main reason the Allies lost against the Japanese were because the Allies were?

    A. out-numbered B. ill-equipped
    C. trapped D. lacked fuel

15. What helped end the Emergency?

    A. Malaya's independence B. Baling talks
    C. Communists emigrating D. Money

16. Under the Anglo-Siamese treaty the Siamese promised not to attack?

    A. Kedah and Perak B. Kedah and Patani
    C. Selangor and Perak D. Selangor and Melaka

17. Who was Malaysia's first Deputy PM?

               A. Ja'afar Onn B. Tun Perak
    C. Tun Razak D. Tunku Abdul Rahman

18. What jobs did the Indian migrants in Malaya generally <u>not</u> do?

               A. police B. fishing
         C. plantation D. railways

19. Which treaty helped create the borders between Malaysia and Indonesia?

    A. Treaty of Bangkok B. Pangkor Treaty
    C. Low Treaty D. Anglo-Dutch treaty

20. Who was the first locally born ruler in Negri Sembilan?

        A. Raja Radin B. Raja Melewar
    C. Yamtuan Antah D. Adityawarman

21. Who fired on the Trengganu fort killing 20 men?

         A. the Siamese B. the British
    C. the Dutch D. Wan Mutahir

22. Which group of people were very loyal to Srivijaya and Melaka?

         A. Javanese B. Sea Gypsies
        C. Ibans D. Semangs

23. Where have cist graves been found?

    A. coastal Kelantan B. Pulau Tioman
    C. Singapore D. southern Perak

24. The British started a settlement in Penang as they no longer wanted to depend on?

    A. Riau-Johor's navy B. the Dutch trade
    C. the Pangkor Treaty D. penal colonies

25. Which was never part of Riau-Johor?

          A. Pahang B. Lingga
       C. Singapore D. Melaka

26. Which group of people arrived first on the Malay peninsula?

    A. Austroasiatics B. Austronesians
      C. Proto-Malays D. Senois

ANSWERS
1.D 2.C 3.C 4.D 5.A 6.B 7.B 8.C
9.C 10.C 11.A 12.A 13.C 14.B 15.A
16.C 17.C 18.B 19.D 20.A 21.B
22.B 23.D 24.B 25.D 26.A

This stone tool is from the palaeolithic age. This was the early part of the Stone Age when primitive stone implements were used. On the Malay peninsula this period was about 34,000 years ago. The tool was discovered at Lenggong, Perak.

Chronology

1st-13th Centuries

1st-5th centuries: The kingdoms of Langkasuka, Kedah, Chi-tu and
    Kiu-li are established on the Malay peninsula.

7th-13th centuries: The Srivijaya Empire from Sumatra is the
    overlord of the Malay peninsula.

13th Century

The Majapahit Empire from Java controls South East Sumatra. The
Ayudhya Empire from Siam has overlordship of the Malay peninsula.

14th Century

1380s Paramesvara flees Palembang for Bintan

About 1390 - Paramesvara rules Singapore

15th Century

About 1400 - Paramesvara founds Melaka

1400 onwards - Minangkabaus begin to migrate to Negeri Sembilan

1404 First Chinese mission to Melaka

1409 Admiral Cheng Ho (Zheng He) visits Melaka

1411 Paramesvara travels to China

1413 Paramesvara dies

1445 Siamese army attacks Melaka

1456-1498 Tun Perak is Bendahara of Melaka

1456 Siamese ships attack Melaka

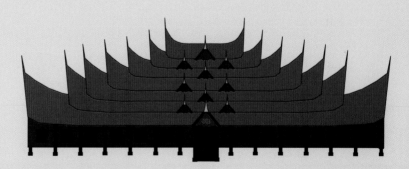

16th Century

1509 The Portuguese arrive in Melaka to trade

1511 The Portuguese attack and conquer Melaka

1515-1524 Sultan Mahmud tries to recapture Melaka but fails

1523 Portuguese attack Kelantan and take slaves

1524 In Sumatra, the Acehnese conquer the kingdom of Pasai

1528 Sultan Mahmud, the last Sultan of Melaka and first Sultan of Riau-Johor, dies in Kampar, Sumatra

1540 Ships from Perak, Siak and Riau-Johor sink 160 Acehnese ships

1551 Sultan Alauddin of Riau-Johor lays siege to Melaka for 3 months

1564 Sultan Alauddin dies as a prisoner in Aceh

17th Century

1629 Aceh attacks Portuguese Melaka with 200 ships and 20,000 men

1629 The Acehnese are defeated by Portuguese and Riau-Johor ships

1634 Riau-Johor sends ship to help Patani fight off the Siamese

1641 The Dutch, with help from Riau-Johor, capture Melaka

1666 War between Riau-Johor and Jambi

1673 The Riau-Johor capital at Batu Sawar is destroyed by Jambi

1677 Raja Ibrahim becomes ruler of Negeri Sembilan and attacks Dutch Melaka with 3000 warriors

1678 Raja Ibrahim of Negeri Sembilan is murdered

1680 Bugis settlement begins in Selangor

1699 Sultan Mahmud, last of the bloodline of Melaka Sultans, is murdered

1699 The Bendahara Abdul Jalil becomes Sultan of Riau-Johor

18th Century

1718 Raja Kechil conquers Riau-Johor and becomes sultan

1721 The Bugis capture Riau-Johor

1721 The Bugis proclaim Sulaiman as Sultan of Riau-Johor

1721 Raja Melewar becomes Yamtuan of Negeri Sembilan

1723-1724 Sultan Muhammad Jiwa of Kedah defeats his younger brother in a civil war

1725 Sultan Zainal Abidin becomes the first Sultan of Trengganu

1733 Sultan Mansur Shah succeeds his father as the Sultan of Trengganu

1746 Raja Kechil dies in Siak, Sumatra

1758 The Bugis are defeated in the first Bugis/Dutch war and Bugis return to Bintan.

1760 Sultan Sulaiman dies

1766 Sultan Salehuddin Shah becomes first Sultan of Selangor

1771 Francis Light meets Sultan Muhammad Jiwa of Kedah

1777 Raja Haji becomes the new Yamtuan Muda in Riau-Johor

1784 The Bugis are defeated in second Bugis/Dutch war

1786 Francis Light starts a British settlement in Penang

1787 The Dutch are chased out of Bintan by Ilanun pirates

1791 Sultan Abdullah of Kedah attacks Penang but fails

1794 Sultan Mansur Shah of Trengganu dies

1795 Britain takes Melaka from the Dutch 'to protect it'

19th Century: *First Half*

1800 Long Muhammad becomes Sultan Muhammad of Kelantan

1809 Patani is broken up by Siamese into seven provinces

1812 Sultan Mahmud III of Riau-Johor dies at Lingga

1812 Kedah helps Siam in its war against the Burmese

1816-1817 Kedah attacks Perak under Siam's orders

1818 Britain gives Melaka back to the Dutch

1819 Raffles starts a British settlement in Singapore

1821 Siam attacks Kedah and Sultan Ahmad Tajuddin flees to Penang

1824 Anglo-Dutch Treaty which divides the Malay world

1825 British gunboats scare off the Siamese fleet sent to attack Perak

1825 Temenggong Abdul Rahman of Singapore dies

1826 Anglo-Siamese Treaty and Low Treaty in Perak

1830 Raja Radin becomes first local born Yamtuan of Negeri Sembilan

1831-1832 The Naning War

1832 The King of Patani is defeated by the Siamese and flees to Kelantan

1835 Sultan Hussein of Singapore dies

1839 The King of Siam appoints Syed Husain Jamalullail chief of Perlis

1839 Baginda Omar becomes the ruler of Trengganu

1839 James Brooke arrives in Sarawak

1841 James Brooke becomes Raja of Sarawak

1842 Sultan Ahmad Tajuddin returns from exile to Kedah

1845 Sayid Husain Jamalullail becomes Raja of Perlis

1848 The chief of Larut, Long Ja'afar, invites the Chinese to mine tin in Larut

19th Century: *Second Half*

1858 Long Ja'afar's son, Ngah Ibrahim, becomes the chief of Larut

1858-1863 Civil War in Pahang

1861 Wan Ahmad of Pahang seeks help from the Siamese King

1862 The Ghee Hin and Hai San gang war in Larut

1862 The fort in Trengganu is shelled by the British

1863 Wan Ahmad becomes the Bendahara of Pahang

1864 Prince Mahmud, former Sultan of Lingga, dies

1865 Charles Moses buys North Borneo from the Sultan of Brunei

1866 Raja Mahdi attacks Kelang

1868 Temenggong Abu Bakar of Johor takes the title of Maharaja

1868 Charles Brooke becomes the second White Rajah of Sarawak

1872 The Ghee Hin and Hai San start fighting again

1873 Yap Ah Loy recovers his Ampang mines from the Ghee Hin

1874 The Pangkor Treaty

1874 Perak, Selangor and Sungei Ujong take a British Resident

1874 Datuk Kelana takes a British Resident in Sungei Ujong

1875 James Birch is killed by Maharaja Lela

1877 Alfred Dent buys North Borneo from the Sultan of Brunei

1878 Yamtuan Antah of Negeri Sembilan is defeated by the British

1881 British North Borneo Company ("Chartered Company")
    established

1885 Maharaja Abu Bakar of Johor takes the title of Sultan

1885 Bendahara Wan Ahmad of Pahang takes the title of Sultan

1885 Spain drops its claim to North Borneo under a treaty

1888 British Treaty with North Borneo and Sultan of Brunei

1888 Pahang takes a British Resident

1891 The British and Dutch draw a border in Borneo

1891-1895 The Pahang war

1895-1905 The Mat Salleh rebellion in North Borneo

1895 Negeri Sembilan is unified under a single British Resident with
    Tuanku Muhammad as the Yamtuan

1896 Perak, Selangor, Negeri Sembilan and Pahang become the
    Federated Malay States

20th Century

1905 The Sultan of Brunei takes a British Resident

1909 The Treaty of Bangkok

1911 The last Sultan of Lingga is removed by the Dutch

1917 Vyner Brooke becomes the third White Rajah of Sarawak

1941 Japan invades British Malaya

1945 The Japanese surrender and the British return to Malaya

1946 Malayan Union proposals

1946 UMNO is formed and Ja'afar Onn becomes their leader

1948 Federation of Malaya

1948-1960 The Malayan Emergency

1951 Sir Henry Gurney is assassinated

1957 Malaya becomes independent

1957 Tunku Abdul Rahman becomes the Prime Minister

1958 Self rule in Singapore

1963 Brunei decides not to join Malaysia

1963 Malaya, Singapore, Sabah and Sarawak join together and form
     a new country – Malaysia

1963 - 1967 Confrontation with Indonesia

1965 Singapore expelled from Malaysia

1969 May 13th racial riots

1970 Tun Abdul Razak becomes the Prime Minister

1976 Tun Hussein Onn becomes the Prime Minister

1981 Tun Mahathir becomes the Prime Minister

1998 The Petronas Twin Towers, the tallest building in the world, is
     built in Kuala Lumpur

21st Century

2003 Abdullah Badawi becomes Prime Minister

2007 Malaysia celebrates its 50th year of independence

2008 Opposition political parties win 5 states in general elections

2009 Najib Tun Razak is to become the next Prime Minister

Glossary

A

Administrators: People who look after public affairs in a town or country.

Agong: see Yang DiPertuan Agong

Allies: The Allies in Malaya included the British, American and Australian forces during World War 2.

Anglo-Dutch Treaty: This 1824 treaty split the Malay world between the English and Dutch.

Anthropologist: a person who studies humankind, especially its many different customs and societies

Archaeological: The study of history and pre-history through digging of sites. The physical remains are examined and may be subject to scientific analysis.

Archipelago: A group of islands. An example is the Riau-Lingga archipelago.

Assassination: To kill a person for political or religious reasons.

B

Batavia: The Dutch trading centre on the island of Java and their seat of government in Asia. The Dutch took it over in 1619, today it is called Jakarta.

Brunei: The kingdom of Brunei used to rule over a great portion of the island of Borneo. Today, Brunei is a small country with a population of about 380,000.

Bendahara: The Chief Minister from the Melaka empire. Later the Bendahara would ruled Pahang as an official for the kingdom of Riau-Johor. In other kingdoms, a Bendahara also acts as the ruler's Chief Minister.

Bidayuhs: Also known as "Land Dayaks", they are a native people of Sarawak. See also Iban.

Borneo: A large island to the east of the Malay peninsula. Today it is divided between the countries of Malaysia and Indonesia. Its name derives from "Brunei".

Bugis: A people from the Celebes (now Sulawesi). They migrated across the Malay archipelago and founded the kingdom of Selangor.

Bunga Mas: Ornamental flowers made of silver and gold. These were given as a tribute by the northern Malay kingdoms to Siam. It showed that Siam was their suzerain or overlord.

C

Chartered Company: The company that ruled over North Borneo until after the Second World War.

Chronology: The arrangement of events in the order in which they occurred.

Colony: A country, territory or settlement which is ruled directly by another country.

Colonial: A period of history when there were colonies in that particular country or region.

Company: A business organisation.

Camphor: A white or transparent solid with an aromatic smell. It is found in the Camphor Laurel tree and was used to make medicine.

Communists: People who want to live in society where all property is owned by the government. There are many forms of Communism.

Coolies: Unskilled labourers

D

Dato': Dato' or Datuk has the same meaning. It literally means "uncle" in Malay. It is also a title used by a chief of a village or district. Today it is an honorary title given to a person by the State or Federal government.

Datuk: see Dato'

Debt-slavery: If a person could not pay his debts he and his family would become slaves to the the person he owed the money to.

Dialect: A form of speech found in another region which is different from the main language spoken in that country.

Dusuns: They are a native people of Sabah.

Dutch: People from the Netherlands, also known as Holland. It was once part of the Habsburg empire.

E

Empire: A country which rules or governs other countries.

Enterprise: A business or difficult job.

Exile: A person forced to be absent from his or her native country.

F

Federated Malay States: The states of Perak, Selangor, Negri Sembilan and Pahang as part of British Malaya.

Federation of Malaya: In 1948, the Federated Malay States, the Unfederated Malay States and the Straits Settlements were joined to form the Federation of Malaya.

G

Garrison: A fortress or the soldiers based in a fortress.

Government: The people or organisation which rules a place. It also refers to a way in which a place is ruled.

Governor: A person who governs a country or region. When governing a colony, he represents the King or Queen of his home country.

I

Iban: Also known as "Sea Dayaks", they are a native people of Sarawak. See also Bidayuh.

Iron Age: A time in the past when people used weapons and tools which were made of iron.

K

Kadazans: They are a native people of Sabah. See also Dusuns.

Kingdom: A country which is ruled in the name of a king or queen.

L

Labuan: A small island near Sabah. It was given to Britain by the Brunei Sultan in 1846. It is today part of Malaysia's Federal Territory.

Langkasuka: An early kingdom on the Malay peninsula, now located in Thailand.

Laksamana: It literally means "Admiral". It is an official position for the Melaka empire.

Lingga: An island at the southern end of the Riau-Lingga archipelago.

Low Treaty: A treaty made between the British and Perak. The British promised to defend Perak against Perak's enemies. Perak gave the island of Pangkor to the British.

M

Mahayana Buddhism: A Buddhist religion born in the 1st century. It is one of the three main Buddhist traditions today.

Malaya: The Malay peninsula, including Singapore. The term came to be used during the British colonial period.

Malaysia: The country is formally known as "The Federation of Malaysia". It is made out of thirteen states: eleven on the peninsula and two in Borneo.

Malay Annals: Also known as *Sejarah Melayu*, these are a collection of stories written about Malay rulers. Created on the command of a Sultan of Melaka, it dates from 1612 and is a literary masterpiece.

Majapahit: An empire from eastern Java which ruled from the 13th century.

Megalith: Large upright stone

Migration: People moving from one place to live in another place

N

Naning: Once a district within Negri Sembilan, today it is part of the state of Melaka.

Niah Caves: It is located near Miri, Sarawak and is part of a national park.

North Borneo: This was the old name for Sabah. Its capital was Jesselton, now renamed as Kota Kinabalu.

O

Orang Laut: Also known as Sea Gypsies, they are an indigenous people who live on in houseboats on the riverine and seas.

Overlord: A higher lord, usually a king which another king has to answer to. Same meaning as a Suzerain.

P

Population: The total number of people living in a location. It also refers to the people generally who live in that location.

Portuguese: People from Portugal. Portugal is in south west Europe and was part of Spain until it became independent in the 12th century.

Portuguese Melaka: The Portuguese conquered Melaka from the Malays and it became a Portuguese trading centre. The Dutch captured Melaka from them 130 years later.

R

Raja: The Raja or Rajah is a ruler of a Malay kingdom. The title Raja is used in modern times for the ruler of Perak. It is an Indian term for Ruler. Raja is also used instead of Tunku or Tengku.

Rajah: see Raja

Rebellion: Armed struggle against the government

Resident: British official in a Malay kingdom. He governs the kingdom in the name of the ruler.

Riau: An island to the north of the Riau-Lingga archipelago. It is close to Singapore. It is also known as Bintan.

Riau-Johor: The new kingdom founded by the Sultan of Melaka after the Portuguese invaded Melaka. The kingdom is also known as Johor Lama or Johor-Riau.

S

Sanskrit: An ancient language from India. It is the basis of many Indian languages including Hindi and Urdu.

Sepoys: An Indian soldier commanded by the British and, originally, led by the East India Company.

Siege: This is when an armed force surrounds an enemy's fort, preventing their escape and cutting off their supplies.

Shah Bandar: The leader of a community for the Melaka empire. There were Shah Bandars for the Chinese, Tamils, Arabs etc.

Siam: The former name for Thailand.

Socio-economic: Society and economy. A society is how a people live their lives. It includes the traditions, believes and customs of a people. An economy is concerned with how people earn a living. It includes the wealth and resources of a community.

Spice Islands: The former name of the islands of the Moluccas. These islands grew cloves, nutmegs, mace and other spices.

Stone Age: A prehistoric time in which weapons and tools were made of stone, bone, wood and other organic material.

Straits Settlements: The British colonies of Penang, Melaka and Singapore.

Settlement: A location which becomes a colony of a foreign power.

Sultan: The ruler of a Malay kingdom. It is an Arab term for ruler.

Suzerain: A kingdom or state that controls another kingdom or state. See also Overlord.

T

Tan Sri: This is an honorary title given to a person by the federal government. It is a higher honour than the 'Datuk' title.

Temenggong: The Chief of Police for the Melaka empire. Later the Temenggong would ruled Johor as an official for the kingdom of Riau-Johor. In other states, a Temenggong is a chief.

Terrorist: A person who uses violence to make demands on the government.

Treaty: An agreement signed between two countries or kingdoms

Tengku: see Tunku

Tun: This is the highest honorary title given to a person by the federal government.

Tunku: Tunku or Tengku has the same meaning, they are just spelled differently in different states. It literally means "prince" but is usually used by those descended from Malay royalty.

U

Unfederated Malay States: The states of Perlis, Kedah, Kelantan, Trengganu and Johor. These states did not have British Residents but Advisors instead.

W

White Rajah: They were the English rulers of Sarawak, beginning with James Brooke in 1868. He was followed by his nephew Charles Brooke and, lastly, Vyner Brooke. Their rule came to an end after the Second World War.

Y

Yang DiPertuan Agong: The king of Malaya and/or Malaysia. The position was created after Malaya's independence in 1957.

Yang DiPertuan Besar: The Malay term for ruler. It is today formally used for the ruler of Negri Sembilan. It is often shortened to Yamtuan

Yang DiPertua Negri: The governor of a state. Since independence, governors were appointed as heads of states for those states without a royal ruler. These are Penang, Melaka, Sabah and Sarawak.

Selected Bibliography

Abdullah Ali. *Malaysian Protocol*. Times Books International, Kuala Lumpur 1986.

Alwi Bin Sheikh Alhady. *Malay Customs and Traditions*. Malaya Publishing House Ltd, Singapore 1962.

Andaya, Barbara Watson & Leonard Y. *A History of Malaysia*. Macmillan Press, London 1982.

Andaya, Leonard Y. Andaya. *The Kingdom of Johor 1641-1728 - Economic and Political Developments*. Oxford University Press, Kuala Lumpur 1975.

Baker, Jim. Crossroads. *A Popular History of Malaysia and Singapore*. Times Books International, Singapore 1999.

Barley, Nigel. *White Rajah*. Time Warner Books UK, London 2002.

Bartlett, Vernon. *Report from Malaya*. Derek Verschoyle Ltd, London 1955.

Bennett, H. Gordon. *Why Singapore Fell*. Angus and Robertson Ltd, Sydney 1944.

Brooke, Sylvia Lady. *Queen of the Head-hunters*. Sidgwick & Jackson, London 1970.

Brown, CC. *Sejarah Melayu or Malay Annals*. Oxford University Press, Petaling Jaya 1970.

Chandriah Appa Rao, Bruce Ross-Larson, Noordin Sopiee, Tjoa Hock Guan. *Issues in Contemporary Malaysia*. Heinemann Educational Books (Asia) Ltd, Kuala Lumpur 1977.

Cheah Boon Kheng, Dr (ed). *The Encyclopedia of Malaysia: Early Modern History 1800-1940*. Editions Didier Millet, Singapore 2001.

Chia, Felix. *The Babas*. Times Books International, Singapore 1980.

Coèdes, George and Damais, Louis-Charles. *Sriwijaya: History, Religion & Language of an Early Malay Polity*. Monograph of the Malaysian Branch Royal Asiatic Society No. 20, Kuala Lumpur 1992.

Collis, Maurice. *Raffles*. Faber and Faber, London 1966.

Crystal, David (editor). *The Cambridge Biographical Encyclopedia*. Cambridge University Press, Cambridge 1999.

Drakard, Jane. *A Kingdom of Words*. Oxford University Press, Shah Alam 1999.

John Leyden's Malay Annals. The Malaysian Branch of the Royal Asiatic Society, Selangor 2001.

German, R.L. *Handbook to British Malaya*. The Malayan Information Agency, London 1927.

Granville-Edge, P.J. *The Sabahan, The Life and Death of Tun Fuad Stephens*. The family of the late Tun Fuad Stephens, Kuala Lumpur 1999.

Gullick, J.M. *A History of Negri Sembilan*. The Malaysian Branch of the Royal Asiatic Society, Selangor 2003.

Gullick, J.M. *Rulers and Residents - Influence and Power in the Malay States 1870-1920*. Oxford University Press, Singapore 1992.

Hall, D.G.E. *A History of South-East Asia*. MacMillan and Company Limited, New York 1966.

Hall, Maxwell. *Labuan Story*. Chung Nam Printing Company, Jesselton 1958.

Ibrahim Syukri (Conner Bailey & John Miksic - translators). *History of The Malay Kingdom of Patani*. Silkworm Books, Chiang Mai 2005.

Kaur, Amarjit. *Historical Dictionary of Malaysia*. The Scarecrow Press Inc, New York 1993.

Kelly, Nigel. *History of Malaya and South-East Asia*. Crescent News (K.L) Sdn Bhd, Selangor 2006.

Kennedy, J. *History of Malaya*, S. Abdul Majeed & Co, Kuala Lumpur 1993.

Khoo Kay Kim. 'The Pangkor Engagement'. Journal of the Malaysian Branch of the Royal Asiatic Society. Volume XLVII Part 1 1974.

Khoo Kay Kim. *Malay Society: Transformation and Democratisation*. Pelanduk Publications, Petaling Jaya 1991.

Lee, H.P. *Constitutional Conflicts in Contemporary Malaysia*. Oxford University Press, USA 1995.

Loeb, Edwin M. *Sumatra, its History and People*. Oxford University Press, Singapore 1972.

Mahathir Mohamad. *The Challenge*. Pelanduk Publications (M) Sdn Bhd. Petaling Jaya, 1986.

Mahathir bin Mohamad. *The Malay Dilemma*. Asia Pacific Press, Singapore 1970.

Majilis Belia Negri Sembilan. *Warisan DiRaja Negri Sembilan Darul Khusus.* Majilis Belia Negri Sembilan.

Miksic, J.N. 'Parallels between the Upright Stones of West Sumatra and those in Malacca and Negri Sembilan'. Journal of the Malaysian Branch of the Royal Asiatic Society. Volume LV111 Part 1 1985.

Miksic, J.N. 'From Seri Vijaya to Melaka Batu Tagak in Historical and Cultural Context'. Journal of the Malaysian Branch of the Royal Asiatic Society. Volume LX Part 2 1987.

Moore, Wendy Khadijah. *Malaysia: A Pictorial History 1400-2004.* Editions Didier Millet, Kuala Lumpur 2004.

Munoz, Paul Michel. *Early Kingdoms of the Indonesian Archipelago and the Malay Peninsula.* Editions Didier Millet Pte Ltd, Singapore 2006.

Nik Hassan Shuhaimi Nik Abdul Rahman (ed), Prof Dato' Dr. *The Encyclopedia of Malaysia: Early History.* Editions Didier Millet, Singapore 1998.

Norhalim Ibrahim. *Negri Yang Sembilan.* Penerbit Fajar Bakti, Shah Alam 1995.

Pelras, Christian. *The Bugis.* Blackwell Press, Massachusetts 1996.

Reid, Anthony (ed). *Indonesian Heritage - Early Modern History.* (Grolier International Inc). Buku Antar Bangsa, Jakarta 1996.

Rentse, Anker. *History of Kelantan.* Journal of the Malayan Branch of the Royal Asiatic Society Vol XII 1934.

Roff, W.R. *The Origins of Malay Nationalism.* University of Malaya Press, Kuala Lumpur 1974.

Shaw, William. *Tun Razak His Life and Times.* Longman Malaysia, Kuala Lumpur 1976.

Sheppard, M.C.ff. 'A Short History of Trengganu' Journal of the Malayan Branch of the Royal Asiatic Society Vol XXII 1949

Sheppard, Mubin. *Tunku – His Life and Times.* Pelanduk Publications, Petaling Jaya, 1995.

Silver, Lynette Ramsay. *The Bridge at Parit Sulong.* Watermark Press 2004.

Slimming, John. *Malaysia: Death of a Democracy.* John Murray, London 1969.

Spruit, Rudd. *The Land of the Sultans: An Illustrated History of Malaysia.* The Pepin Press BV, Amsterdam 1995.

Stewart, Brian. *Smashing Terrorism in the Malayan Emergency*. Pelanduk Publications, Subang Jaya 2004.

Suwannathat-Pian, Kobkua. *Thai-Malay Relations - Traditional Intra-regional Relations from the Seventeenth to the Early Twentieth Centuries*. Oxford University Press 1992.

Tan-Wong, Nellie S.L and Patel, Vipin (ed). *Adat Perpatih*. Wintrac (WWB/Malaysia) Sdn Bhd, Kuala Lumpur 1992.

Tun Salleh Abbas with K.Das. *May Day for Justice*. Promarketing Publications, Kuala Lumpur 1989.

Tunku Abdul Rahman. *As a Matter of Interest*. Heinemann Educational Books (Asia) Pty Ltd. Petaling Jaya, 1981.

Tunku Abdul Rahman. *Something to Remember*. Eastern Universities Press, Singapore 1983.

Tunku Abdul Rahman. *Lest We Forget*. Eastern Universities Press Sdn Bhd, Petaling Jaya, 1983.

Tunku Abdul Rahman. *Looking Back - The Historic Years of Malaya and Malaysia*. Pustaka Antara, Kuala Lumpur 1977.

Tunku Abdul Rahman. *Viewpoints*. Heinemann, Kuala Lumpur 1978.

Tunku Halim. *A Children's History of Malaysia*. Pelanduk, Subang Jaya 2003.

Tunku Halim. *Tunku Abdullah - A Passion for Life*. All-Media Publications Sdn Bhd, Kuala Lumpur 1998.

Turnbull, C. Mary. *A Short History of Malaysia, Singapore and Brunei*. Graham Brash, Singapore 1980.

Wang Gungwu (ed). *Malaysia: A Survey*, F.W. Cheshire, Melbourne 1964.

Winstead, Richard. *Malaya and its History*, Hutchinson & Co, London 1958.

Winstead, Richard, *The Malays - A Cultural History*, Routledge & Kegan Paul, London 1956.

Winstead, Richard. *A History of Johore (1365-1941)*. Malayan Branch of the Royal Asiatic Society Reprint of Journal of the Malayan Branch of the Royal Asiatic Society 1932 & 1979. Kuala Lumpur 1992.

Zakaria Haji Ahmad, Prof Dato' Dr (ed). *The Encyclopedia of Malaysia: Government and Politics*. Editions Didier Millet, Singapore 2006.

Index

Picture Credits

Many of the photographs for this book were taken at different museums in Malaysia. The Author is very grateful to the following organisations:

> *Galeri Sultan Azlan Shah, Kuala Kangsar, Perak*
> *Lembah Bujang Archaeology Museum, Merbok, Kedah*
> *Taiping Museum, Taiping, Perak*
> *Muzium Negara, Kuala Lumpur*
> *Muzium Tentara Darat, Port Dickson, Negri Sembilan*
> *Akrib Negara Malaysia*

Author
pages: 3-13 14M 14B 16-18 19M 21 23B 24L 24M 26 28M 28B 29B 30 32B 33B 34 35B 36 37M 38-44 45T 46B 47M 48T 50M 52 53M 55-57 59T 60T 60M 61 62 63R 66 67M 68 69R 71B 73 76 77T 78 79 80T 82L 84 85L 85R 86 87M 88 89M 90 91 93M 93B 95T 95L 96 96T 98 99T 100-103 106-118 130-133

Suzanne Best *pages*: 60R 100

Tunku Yahaya *pages*: 53T 64L

Bingley Sim *pages*: 144

Sally McAteer
pages: 1 14T 15B 22 24R 27 28T 31T 37T 45T 54M 65R 71T 71M 72 74 75M 81 83 85B 91T 92 93T 99M 104 120 124 127 129

T=Top B=Bottom L=Left R=Right M=Middle

141

The Children's Home of Hope

With every purchase of this book the author is donating RM5.00 to the Children's Home of Hope, which is is part of the **National Cancer Society of Malaysia**.

Children's Home of Hope

The home provides accommodation for children who are receiving cancer treatment. Established in 1996, the home is at Bangunan Persatuan Kebangsaan Kanser at 66, Jalan Raja Muda Abdul Aziz, Kuala Lumpur. Most importantly, it is within walking distance from the hospital.

It is a "home away from home" for it allows children receiving cancer treatment to stay at this home with their family.

National Cancer Society of Malaysia

The charity was founded in 1966 and is financed entirely by voluntary contributions from the public and receives no government funding. The Society is dedicated to preventing cancer, saving lives from cancer and improving the quality of life of those living with cancer through patient care and education.

For further information:

http://www.cancer.org.my
Email: contact@cancer.org
Tel:+6 03 - 2698 7300
Fax:+6 03 - 2698 4300

"The best chance of fighting the disease of cancer is through education and early diagnosis."

National Cancer Society Malaysia

To make your gift

Name : _____   E-mail : _____

Phone No: H: _____   H/p: _____   Office: _____

Company: _____

Contact Person: _____

Address: _____

_____   Postcode: _____   State: _____

1) How did you hear about the National Cancer Society of Malaysia?

✔ **Encyclopedia**   ○ Brochure   ○ Friend/family
○ Website   ○ Newspaper   ○ **NCSM Client**

2) Which type of donation would you like to make would you like?

○ Unconditional Gift   ○ **Children's Home of Hope**
○ Memorial Gift *(honours memory of a loved one)*   ○ Other *(please state)* _____

3) Amount you wish to donate: RM: _____

○ **Directly into Maybank (Main)**   Acc. No:0-14011-4-30448

○ **Money Order/Postal Order** _____

○ **Cheque**   No: _____
All donations to be made payable to ' National Cancer Society of Malaysia'

○ **Credit card.** Please debit my Credit card number

| | | | | | | | | | | | | | | | | Expiry date ____ / ____

Card Type *(e.g. Visa/Mastercard/American Express)* _____

Cardholder's name *(as it appears on credit card)* _____

Signature

All donations to be made payable to 'National Cancer Society of Malaysia'

Please send your donation and this form to:
The National Cancer Society of Malaysia, P.O.Box 12187, 50770 Kuala Lumpur

Please include your name and postal address to ensure we can mail a receipt to you.
Thank you for your donation, a receipt will be sent to you shortly.

If you would like to make a donation, please photocopy this page. Then fill out the photocopied form above and post it to the National Cancer Society of Malaysia, together with your donation.

About the Author

Publishing this book has been a five-year labour of love for the author. Other than conceiving, researching and writing this encyclopedia, he is also responsible for its design, page layout, original photography, image manipulation, illustrating all maps and diagrams and most illustrations.

Tunku Halim was born in 1964. He was educated in St. John's in Malaysia and in Cheltenham College, Sussex University and The City University in England. He holds a Masters degree with Distinction in Shipping, Trade and Finance and is a Barrister of the Inner Temple. He has been admitted as a solicitor in Malaysia and New South Wales.

He has written numerous collections of short stories, novels, a biography and is the author of *A Children's History of Malaysia*.

Other than writing, his other passions are property investment, design and development. His other interests include Yoga and Pilates. He is also a black belt in three Karate styles. He is married to Suzanne and has two children, Kristina and Adam. This encyclopedia is dedicated to them.

The author can be contacted at tunkuhalim@gmail.com and has a blog at http://tunkuhalim.wordpress.com.

Acknowledgments

I would like to thank my wife, Suzanne Best, for her support and understanding as I created this encyclopedia. I am grateful to my friend, Bingley Sim, who accompanied me on my photographic expeditions. I also wish to thank my illustrator, Sally McAteer, for her good work. I am indebted to Wong Pek Lin and Francis Wong who have, once again, lent me many reference books. I am grateful to Dato' Ng Tieh Chuan whom, through MPH Group Publishing and Pelanduk Publications, has published twelve of my thirteen previous books. I would also like to thank Eric Forbes for his diligent editing of almost all of my previous efforts.

I am deeply grateful to my late father, Tunku Tan Sri Abdullah, whose generosity has allowed me the time to create this encyclopedia. It was also by writing his biography, which was published over a decade ago, that sparked my interest in Malaysian history. I would also like to thank Dato' Abdul Ghani Mohamed Nor whom through my childhood years has been a bastion of support and has always encouraged reading.

Lastly, I am indebted to you Dear Reader for your interest in this book and in Malaysia's fascinating history. History is about stories, real stories. These true tales have much to teach us about where we have been, where we are now and where we are going to ...